I0568332

AN EDUCATIONAL JOURNEY AGAINST ALL ODDS IN GUYANA SOUTH AMERICA

In Guyana South America Experience the Journey-The Struggles-The Triumphs

ADARSH KUMAR HARI

Copyright @2022 by Adarsh Kumar Hari

All rights reserved. No part of this book may be reproduced in any form or by any electronic or mechanical means, including information storage and retrieval systems, without permission in writing from the publisher, except by reviewers, who may quote brief passages in a review.

This publication contains the opinions and ideas of its author. It is intended to provide helpful and informative material on the subjects addressed in the publication. The author and publisher specifically disclaim all responsibility for any liability, loss or risk, personal or otherwise, which is incurred as a consequence, directly or indirectly, of the use and application of any of the contents of this book.

WORKBOOK PRESS LLC
187 E Warm Springs Rd,
Suite B285, Las Vegas, NV 89119, USA

Website: https://workbookpress.com/
Hotline: 1-888-818-4856
Email: admin@workbookpress.com

Ordering Information:
Quantity sales. Special discounts are available on quantity purchases by corporations, associations, and others.
For details, contact the publisher at the address above.

Library of Congress Control Number:
ISBN-13:   978-1-956876-95-6 (Paperback Version)
                                (Digital Version)

REV. DATE: 10/03/2022

CONTENTS

ACKNOWLEDGEMENTS

The writing of this book did require a great deal of research and data acquisition. I am indeed fortunate and most thankful to have the written contributions of the many former students and teachers whose educational journeys and success stories are hereby reported in this book.

For other invaluable information and materials on these schools (RHS, PMCI and CCHS),I would like to specially thank the following persons: Jai Seecharran and his wife, Chandra, Sagar Sanichar, Haripersaud (Brazo), Ray Sundar, Julip Singh, Bansraj Mangru and his wife, Joyce, Jagat James, Dr. Leila Mangru, Ganesh Harilall, Chandradutt Madhoo, Mohanlall Birbahadur and the many others who directly or indirectly were helpful in so many ways.

My special thanks to Chunmattie Gurbatur, for her support and encouragement.

A special thanks to Errol Arthur for his feedback and special contributions on important issues of the book.

A heartfelt thanks to Daniel Laughery for his helpfulness with the computer.

I must remember also, my very dear friend, Nolan Greer, for his genuine feedback throughout the long haul of my writing this book.

Also, to Terry Ford and Ursula Willing, my special thanks for their wonderful support in this venture.

Most of all, my sincerest gratitude goes to my dearest wife, Lee, for her total unflinching support, encouragement and inspiration she gave me in making this undertaking possible.

FOREWORD

I have known Adarsh Kumar Hari for many years. It was during this period when we both served with the Houston Independent School District, Texas that we developed a close affinity. Besides his friendship, I discerned that Adarsh was genuinely interested in the field of education. Adarsh's travels, from his birthplace at Uitvlugt, West Coast Demerara, to the Corentyne, Berbice then to Minnesota in the United States and later to Houston, Texas and finally to San Antonio, Texas where he retired as a successful commercial real estate agent, revealed to us an intriguing itinerary. At these diverse locations, he engaged in educational pursuits. Adarsh's journeys and activities exemplify the spirit of entrepreneurship and altruism.

In Corentyne Berbice, Adarsh was a member of the trio, Rudra Nath and Udai Panday being the other two that founded the Rose Hall High School which later merged with Port Mourant Comprehensive Institute to form the Corentyne Comprehensive High School. At these institutions, Adarsh experienced the fulfillment of his childhood dreams – the academic success of disadvantaged students of the locality during his ten - year tenure there.

Adarsh's years of exemplary service came to fruition when he witnessed at first hand the advancement of his students in various fields of endeavor and their contribution to their respective communities.

I applaud Adarsh for revealing his sojourns and experiences to us. Apart from his own academic achievement; he was awarded both the Bachelor's and Master's degrees from the University of Winona, Minnesota. He must be complimented for performing one of his greatest acts of charity by sharing his wealth, knowledge and wisdom with his fellowmen. Adarsh continues to support the education of students in his native country as well as in the United States.

I highly commend his memoirs to the discriminating reader.

Krishna Singh

M.Ed. (Ed. Psy.); BSc. Econ.) Hons.

PREFACE

I have to say my reflections of Rose Hall High School and Corentyne Comprehensive High School were great journey of changes. Changes that were brought about by former students and teachers at these institutions. The odds were against them, and through it all I can still visualize the efforts and accomplishments that had taken place in order to reach their extraordinary goals. Yet, there is no greater good but to celebrate our achievements and fully embrace success experienced in the end.

The narratives that are written by the students and teachers explain a vivid journey of challenges and successes worth the legacy inherited. It is a pleasure to be introduced to their unique experiences that capture every emotional detail. This tour into their lives will give all readers an insight into the development, growth, challenges, progression and successes, detail by detail.

It is incredibly fulfilling to be a part of these great institutions that have so improved or helped serve students and teachers to their unselfish goals. It's within these institutions that it was made possible to create an educational foundation for others. It was the intellectually acquired resources that made their vision possible. It ultimately enables our students and teachers to become competitive and successful in today's world.

It is with great joy that I dedicate this book and acknowledge:

1. All participants who have lifted and established the educational banner of these institutions.

2. Rudra Nath, the founder and pioneer of Rose Hall High School, who has provided the avenue for

achievements to all participants.

3. John Muria, another pioneer of extraordinary vision was the founder of Port Mourant Comprehensive Institute which after the merger with Rose Hall High School became Corentyne Comprehensive High School. Furthermore, when these schools were acquired by the Guyana government – free education became available to all high school students......A LEGACY THAT WILL LIVE ON.

INTRODUCTION

When I turn the pages of time in my mind and visualize the decades of changes time brought through our affiliation with Rose Hall High School, Port Mourant Comprehensive Institute and Corentyne Comprehensive High Schools I come to realize that these changes were very significant indeed in our lives.

These Institutions gave us a grand opportunity that inspired us with a stronger will, a better hope, a renewed strength and the required groundwork that enabled us to be successful in all our endeavors. Indeed, we were motivated to do better because we saw that it was wise and was the right thing to do in our aspiration to achieve greater educational successes and to reach unattainable heights.

In the forthcoming chapters, we will see how some of the students and teachers have captured their most wonderful challenges and the opportunities facing them. These individuals among others have been the eyewitnesses to all of the challenges, hardships, and changes that occurred and have brought now their shared experiences, and have given us their outstanding contributions, as well as their remarkable successes that left us a legacy with each role so uniquely different, yet, superbly outstanding.

Looking at these remarkable journeys of these hard-working students and these dedicated teachers, we feel a sense of awe and admiration towards them. We feel in our hearts a sense of gratitude for their dedication and commitment. Yes, these are the characters who have now bequeathed to us their gifts of sacrifice and commitment and achievements and who now remind us that this journey of life is significantly worthy of living.

A Poem on The Schools (RHS, PMCI and CCHS)

By Adarsh Kumar Hari

The echoing sounds of education vibrated far and wide;

The diverse needs of our children sounded, but were somewhat denied.

Then, in '58, to this cause came three –Rudra, Hari and Panday,

their motto, 'education for all' ,'twas a message meant to stay.

In Rose Hall Village, RHS was the school we waited to see.

Rock Diamond was converted and a new institution came to be.

For each child the projected goal was a good education

gained only by study, sacrifice, hard work, and dedication.

Here, our super teachers and students worked hard together,

And soon their desired successes were achieved easier.

Our students' grades at the C.P. Exam were superbly good,

emphasis was on 'study', and this they understood.

After two years we outgrew the school we were then renting.

On 3 ac. land in the 'swamp' a new school we planned on building.

To meet the demands of this outstanding institution

funds were collected from concerts and from house- to -house collection.

From the teachers, students, and yes, from the community

Through their dedication, sacrifice, hard work and unity,

our concrete building (120x33) was finally complete.

Every measure of accomplishment we were able to meet.

It seemed we had everything our high school would need:

a caring principal, superb teachers, and great students, indeed.

Our 'Senior' and 'GCE' results were demonstrably outstanding;

Yet, we strove to do more and to do better, with time revealing.

Progress was recognized in every ventured direction

In sports, in debates and other areas of education.

Our success story was highlighted in every way;

RHS was greatly admired –'twas the talk of the day.

Then Rudra created the Board of Governors –t'was his free choice.

Thought this would bring to RHS a more outstanding voice.

At first, things went well; there was mutual admiration.

Then, dissensions arose on finance and administration.

A court order (an injunction) against Rudra was served;

he was to keep out of RHS. Yes, his cries went unheard.

Rudra then found refuge at the Port Mourant Pavilion,

and our disrupted school rested in this new location.

Moving to the Race Course from Rose Hall swamp, (the reef)

Brought to us countless changes as we turned a new leaf;

our will was strong and our determination steadfast

and solutions to our problems we soon learned fast.

We stayed there several months as our struggles endured.

We made great progress and undoubtedly, we felt secure;

Rudra then announced that a merger was scheduled to be.

This merger to become CCHS we finally did see.

This welcome merger brought to both school's great stability;

yet, there were problems as to who holds top priority.

Soon, our ship of education was sailing a calmer sea.

Unity, progress and exam results were our top priority.

Rudra then left and Ramdehol joined our great institution.

He made many reforms and improvements –t'was his contribution.

We experienced more growth during his administration,

In cricket, table tennis, debates and, in education.

Ramdehol then left and Kesrielall joined the train

with CCHS undergoing more changes again.

Then, the Guyana Government brought the final conversion

and CCHS received free secondary education.

The journey of RHS, PMCI and CCHS spanned 12 years or more;

there were challenges, successes, and experiences galore.

We saw growth, development, and great achievements, too,

from these superb institutions, and a legacy that's true.

CHAPTER 1

RUDRA NATH VISITS THE CORENTYNE

Rudra Nath had conceived a plan to start a high school in the Corentyne Berbice area. He, together with a friend, Vivek Mohanram, visited the Corentyne area. During a meeting with R.N. Persaud, the Principal of R.N. High School, R.N. Persaud was very pleased with Rudra concerning this venture and suggested to him that it was a very noble and laudable plan to open another high school-- one that was much needed in the area, and that Rose Hall Village was the ideal location to establish a new high school.

In the fall of 1958 three pioneers, Rudra Nath, Udai Panday, and Adarsh Hari, who themselves were educators, set out on a mission to found the Rose Hall High School (RHS) in Rose Hall Village, Corentyne, Berbice. Here an institution was born. Several factors favored this location: geographic, economic and social.

Rose Hall Village was strategically located between the town of New Amsterdam and Skeldon sugar estate. The Village was sandwiched between two very productive major sugar estates – Pl. Albion in the East and Port Mourant in the West. Port Mourant is the birthplace of the great political leader, the Honorable, Dr. Cheddi Jagan, former President of Guyana. In addition, Rose Hall Village is intersected by a major roadway that connects New Amsterdam and goes right through this Village ending at Skeldon. This major roadway also connects all the other farms and villages from New Amsterdam on the west to Crabwood Creek on the eastern tip of Guyana.

Rose Hall Village was also important economically. It boasted itself of major attractive centers and institutions, like banks, post office, grocery and other retail stores, restaurants, barber shops, and beauty salons, a cinema, a drugstore, a temple and a mosque. There were also elementary schools, private high schools, and other attractions that catered to the needs of the people of Rose Hall Village, as well as the surrounding estates and other neighboring villages. Rose Hall Village prides itself as a major confluence to all the major areas in the Corentyne area. The people of Rose Hall Village are very proud of their village; a good many of them own their own businesses. Many of the villagers are professionals – doctors, lawyers, school teachers, etc., and they play great roles in what's going on in their village in matters of politics, education, and social interests.

The people of Rose Hall Village are also very friendly and sociable. The village attracted many social activities. The Rock Diamond hotel, before it was converted to Rose Hall High School, was a very popular, social and entertainment center. They were also several social events that captivated the hearts of the villagers – so much to see and so much to do. They found entertainment at the Apollo Cinema, classy dining restaurants, concerts and a host of other attractions. Shopping is a unique every day event as people from the nearby estates and villages, as well as from Rose Village itself, would do their shopping in the stores that are on both sides of the major roadway. Rose Hall Village prided itself as having the most attractive stores in the Corentyne area. Stores like Alim Shaw, the Abdools, the Ramjohns (they were the ones who leased Rock Diamond hotel to Rudra), from which we started our Rose Hall High School; the Dharrys, Coppin, Zaman --just to name a few. Also, the open air market in the village is another major attraction where vegetables and fruits and fresh fish are brought daily to the market.

Rose Hall Village is also very unique for its Christmas Eve special-an event that made this village come alive as residents, families, friends, and visitors parade the streets of Rose Hall celebrating Christmas Eve by just coming out and enjoying the evening. This major roadway is extremely busy with this collective and spirited group of celebrants. Here they do their special Christmas shopping, buying special items for themselves and loved ones or just enjoy window shopping. The shoppers are happy to have the best and most famous stores from which to choose. It is always noteworthy to see that Rose Hall Main Street becomes transformed into a night of lights and decorations. The stores are decorated each in their own unique way, yet, each produces a special and vibrant attraction. People also find themselves visiting the restaurants and enjoying fine dining. Some would enjoy special treats at the Harris' shop, treating themselves to the special ice cream treats of so many varieties or the many confectionaries and cakes of quite a variety, including, the famous, 'pine-tart,' the 'Chinese cake' and the 'black-eye', on display in his store. There were many other specialties such as milk shakes, soft drinks and sodas. They would also find themselves just enjoying the delicious apples and grapes of the Christmas season. This season surely lifts the spirits of the celebrants and seemingly everyone joyously enjoys a wonderful and memorable evening.

One other factor that attributed to Rose Hall being an excellent choice was that the primary schools and private high schools were not able to meet the surging and the demanding needs of the children looking for greater opportunities towards higher education. Because of these many attractive features Rose Hall Village was selected as the ideal place for our school.

CHAPTER 2

THE BIRTH OF ROSE HALL HIGH SCHOOL AT ROCK DIAMOND

THIS IS WHERE IT ALL STARTED

THIS IS A PHOTO OF THE "ROCK DIAMOND HOTEL" WHICH WAS LATER CONVERTED TO "ROSE HALL HIGH SCHOOL".

(COURTESY OF LILLMAN DWARKA).

The three pioneers, although they knew what they had in mind, were unaware of the challenges and sacrifices that they would have to make. Yet, they believed that to succeed there must be hard work, dedication, and commitment, as well as the required motivation coupled with an undaunted spirit. A good location was paramount.

Rudra Nath and Hafiz Ramjohn, the new owner of Rock Diamond hotel, entered into a mutual lease agreement. The Rock Diamond hotel, long established as a hotel and entertainment center, was quickly converted to a new image – the Rose Hall High School.

Our next step was to get the new place ready. Mr. Lakraj from Letter Kenny volunteered to make desks, benches and blackboards and donated these to our new school. Mr. Noor Mohammed and his crew also helped with the construction by removing walls and creating new classrooms. Soon, recruiting students to our school was our next big step.

We found that the majority of the students were poor financially. In addition, these students faced further deprivation when they could not meet the educational requirements set by the other institutions of learning in the neighborhood. Besides, very many of these students were too old to attend high schools – they were over 18 years. We were there to help as our resounding motto was "education for all "--a banner that flew its message for every child regardless of who he or she was.

We started Rose Hall High School in the fall of 1958. Rudra and I decided to live in the school building for a while. He occupied one of the towers; and I took the other one. This was financially helpful to us and on reflection it was the best thing that happened to us.

Our first patch of students numbered 14 and as our numbers increased we had to create other classrooms to accommodate these new students. Soon, we were recruiting more students from the neighboring areas: Port Mourant, Belvedere, Albion, Fyrish, and other surrounding areas. We were very glad to welcome new students no matter who they were or from where they came. Yes, no matter what their background affiliations were – social, religious, political, economic, etc. – we were proud to be there for them. We were happier to learn that our principal, Rudra, gave a lending ear and a helping hand to all those children in dire need and who could not afford to attend high school. Rudra was very kind and considerate. He gave many children free and partial tuition depending on the needs of these children. Rudra did not discriminate among his students-- he treated all alike. Some of the Afro-Guyanese students who could not afford school fees ($18.00 per semester) were also given free tuition.

It did not take very long to see our small classrooms grew rapidly from 14 to 40 and then to 70. Soon, we were boasting a total number of 200 students and in less than two years our enrollment peaked to about 250 students. While our student enrollment grew in numbers our teachers also increased. By this time, we had occupied the entire upper floor of the building as well as a part of the lower building. It must be noted here that there was not much space for recreation or lunch areas for the students. Lunch had to be taken by many of our students in the classrooms or in areas in front of the building or at the back of the building while others would go to nearby shops to have a snack or just do window shopping. Noisy traffic, dust and other distractions were major setbacks we faced. Our motto for our school, as stated earlier, was to educate every child and to bring out the best in each child despite the challenges and setbacks we were facing. We tried our best to help them do better by encouragement, motivation, and being there for them by working through their weaknesses and giving them support in areas needed. Thus, we were influencing these students towards higher achievements. It would be worthy to note that we took great pride in whatever we did, and despite our educational inadequacies we were always gathering educational data to enrich our teaching techniques. The key factor that helped us in this initial period was that we were constantly communicating with each other. Rudra and the teachers were always finding ways to promote education. We were organizing, recruiting and implementing new ideas and strategies for the classroom. Also, we were brainstorming the best course of action that would facilitate and advance learning for our students. Rudra would encourage and support the teachers and would help in every way he could to build self-confidence, harmonize teacher-teacher relationships, student-teacher relationships as well as advance those techniques that would promote learning.

By helping the students realize their goals, we found that the higher we set our standards, these students (with few exceptions) transcended our expectations. We were there helping them to achieve their true potential. Many of our students were given accelerated promotions allowing them to advance to the next higher grade level. Surprisingly, these students were able to compete with the other students at that level and in all cases did outstandingly well. In fact, in 1961 Rudra was getting a group of our students ready for the College of Preceptors Exam.

This Exam was administered by the University of London, England and it was designed to promote sound learning as well as to provide a good education system for students at the Secondary education level. Certificates were awarded to qualified candidates. As it turned out many of our graduates (those who left school) were successful in finding gainful employment in the public as well as the private sectors of the workforce.

Rudra did not have enough students to sit for the Exam. He recruited the best of the students from the lower forms to make up 50 students. We realized that this was a great challenge; some schools had to prepare their students for three years or more before their students could be ready to write this C.P. Exam. Our students had only two years of preparation. We decided to push them to the hilt using every measure to get them ready towards the anticipated goal. We were giving them as much teaching exercises as possible, giving them lots of motivation and instilling confidence in them and allowing them to believe and work harder so that they would do better. We were also concentrating on lifting the standards of the weaker students. Finally, our students were ready, and they were able to take the Exam. The results were stunning. We celebrated with 90% passes with outstanding grades of A's and B's.

Through the kind courtesy of Chunmattie Gurbatur, one of the fifty students of the first batch that wrote the College of Preceptors Exam -- the class of 1960, I herby reproduce the names of those students.

STUDENT ROSTER AT THE CP EXAM

Austin, Ormin	Samaroo, Harinarine
Permaul, Arjoonan	Sharma, Kirajpat
Bachan, Deodat	Khan, Azim
Persaud, Dwarka	Sharma, Madawachari
Baksh, Rahim	Khuba, Bhawani S.
Persaud, Kampta	Seetaram, Suresh
Balgobin, Haripersaud	Lakraj, Jaisook
Persaud, Kesso	Singh, Indal
Bangaroo, Venus	Mangra, John
Punwasie, Hardatt	Singh, Kaisree

Birbahadur, Mohanlall

Ramdehol, Isardutt

Bissessar, Dorris

Ramjohn, Shereen

Chapman, Lawrence

Ramroop, Hansram

Chisolm, Henry

Ramsagar, Kamal

Chunoo, Ganpat

Ramsaroop, Melvin

DeGroot, Vera

Ramdeo, Rampertab

Evans, Marsha

Ramkumar, Janmawattie

Ramcharran, Haridatt

Mann, Clifford

Singh, Tyrone

Mangru, Rohini

Sukhai, Peter

Munilall, Baliram

Surujlall, Apsalamadin

Nandnan, Parasar

Thomas, Sydney

Nansram, Hilton

Williams, Hugh

Permaul, Stanley

Wood, James

Ramatullah, Hussein

Gurbatur, Yachumattie

Samaroo, Harinarine

Our school's popularity became very much widespread which had a resounding effect on our student population. We were definitely experiencing a tremendous surge in our new enrollment. In addition to the run of the day classes, we also catered classes for adults in the evening. It was a means to accommodate the needs of those who needed to advance their education but who worked during the day.

CHAPTER 3

ROSE HALL HIGH SCHOOL RELOCATION TO THE SWAMP (REEF)

THIS WAS THE ORIGINAL ROSE HALL HIGH SCHOOL AT REEF THAT WAS BUILT BY TEACHERS, STUDENTS, AND THE COMMUNITY (NOTE THE CRABGRASS, A NATIVE WEED, THAT GROWS AT THE SWAMP)

(COURTESY OF VINCE RAMCHARAN)

This school we were in was now too small for our rapidly growing population. Under Rudra's guidance and management, it was decided that we should build our new school in another area of Rose Hall Village called the 'swamp,' a low-lying land in Rose Hall.

This venture was a big operation and required tremendous efforts. However, two operatives aided us in this venture. One was the name of our school. Rose Hall High School was becoming a household name, due to the fact we were producing great results. The other factor was that Rudra was seen as well respected and trusted. He was seen as a person of honesty, integrity, and dependability.

With Rudra's ingenious efforts, and with help from the students and teachers, as well as support from the community, we were set on a fund raising mission. We started from our base, Rose Hall Village and travelled as far as Canji and Skeldon; about a 60-mile distance from both sides of Rose Hall Village. Our mission was to visit every home and gather whatever monetary contributions were given and at the same time educate the public about our new school and its goals. We tried to encourage the parents to have a more open mind and to meet the needed and more realistic call of educating the girls in their families. It seems, however, that this new concept was gradually taking effect. The parents were still locked in their old mode of thinking that girls do not need to have an education. Money also came from rich donors and even from our own staff members. Money also came from the concerts we were sponsoring. Our concerts were really grand and entertaining. We were aided by the popular bands of the day -- The Dil Bahar Orchestra and the Diana Orchestra. We travelled across the Corentyne area wooing the inhabitants to a night of fun and merriment usually on Saturday nights. Their music and songin 1963facilities s were always a hit - very sentimental, romantic, and very entertaining to the audience.

The concerts were usually opened by Adarsh, who with his popular song 'oh Guyana...' captivated the audience with his charming, and powerful voice-- a sample of allowing the audience to know what was in store for them. We had fabulous entertainers like Henry who created quite a sensation with his song, 'Oh, Bangali Baboo'. We were also being serenaded by the voices of Boni Persaud, Ramjit Bhajan and Jack Bhajan. However, we could never forget the haunting melody of Premchand Dass and Shanti Budhram as they sang their famous duet 'Dekh a may awaz na dena'. Then, we were captivated by the accordion, wonder boy, Dindial Jagnandan, who was tantalizing and captivating with his many musical renditions. Other singers included our very own Liloutie Ramteg and Somatie Ramtege who, every time they sang, cast a magic spell on our audience with their soothing, yet, haunting melodies. Then, there was James Wood, who mesmerized his audience with his great impersonation of Johnny Mathis. Lawrence Chapman also was quite entertaining with his contributions. But, it was Ivan Harry who brought the audience to rollicking laughter with his comical entertaining features. We were further entertained by other entertainers, particularly, Joseph Chinapen with his comical yet dramatic sketches. Also, we could not forget the group entertainers, including our own, Jagat James as they sang and danced their way into the hearts of the audience. Then, after a little bit more of fun and entertainment, the audience was ready to hear from special guest speakers including some of our teachers followed by our chieftain, Rudra Nath, who captivated the audience with more interesting data and highlights about our school.

This exercise of collecting money from house- to- house and doing concerts was not an easy task, but this undertaking was essentially important as this cause was very significant and worthy. After we had collected enough money, we were ready to start construction of our new school. Help came from several sources. Cecil Ramoo was the chief contractor in charge of the construction of the school. He had a tremendous workforce of dependable and expert workers. It was he who made and donated desks and chairs to our new school. There was also Noor Mohammad, another contractor with his team of experts who assisted in the construction phase. In addition to these teams, there were lots of volunteers who assisted in this big venture.

To build the school required months and months of hard work, dedication, sacrifice and much capital. The efforts were through a long and intensive self-help undertaking in which every step was carefully monitored to ensure safety and thoroughness while still meeting the required codes and regulations of Rose Hall Village. We worked during the days into the evenings, sometimes seven days a week. In the evenings and into the nights we worked with the help of a small lighting plant that Rudra provided.

Once the land was fully ready for construction, we had the concrete foundation poured. Concrete blocks for the building were made by volunteers of the community, by the workers of Cecil Ramoo and those of Noor Mohammed, plus several teachers and students of our school. The efforts of our teachers and students were extraordinary. They participated in all phases of construction and in this endeavor, surprisingly, we cannot recall any moment when they complained. They were unrelenting, determined and dedicated. Here we saw unity at its best, and here we saw that although their hands were blistered, and even sometimes bloodied with the heavy labor of construction, and even when the sun was 80-90 degrees Fahrenheit these superstars of loyalty never complained. Day after day and even during the evenings, we sometimes saw the same faces ready to give more of themselves to this great task. This sacrifice came about because of their love and devotion and towards a worthy cause. After more than a year, this gigantic ordeal, what seemed to be an endless operation, came to a partial completion.

Having achieved this almost impossible task we were at last able to see our former school transferred its students (an amount of 250) to this new location. What an accomplishment! After we moved to this new location, we continued to build the remaining unfinished part of the building, which took about another five months by way of the same self-help undertaking.

Our students found the climate of their new school, after a long wait, as ideal. We had a great office for teachers, one for the principal, and an office comfortable for the secretary, Ms. Butcher. Then, we added a library to encourage reading and to be used as a reference center. We had a large recreational outdoor area for games and outdoor activities, and even our toilet facilities were better.

IN 1963 AT ROSE HALL HIGH SCHOOL (REEF), THE LIBRARY, AN INTERGRAL PART OF OUR EDUCATIONSYSTEM, WAS ESTABLISHED, (COURTESY OF BRAZO HARIPERSAUD)

While our students and teachers were getting accommodated to their new environment, however, because of the need for additional funds for construction, we extended our usual visitations to other areas on our money collection campaign and continued with our grand concerts while educating the people about our school. During this period (1961-1962), our enrollment had peaked to about 400 students and the number of our teachers rose to 25. We were experiencing a tremeupcomndous explosion in our enrollment as students were coming from near and far to our new building. The opening of the Black Bush Polder (BBP) settlement by the PPP government, during Dr. Cheddi Jagan's administration, created an attractive environment for the children who wanted to attend high school but who could not gain admittance in the secondary high schools in the areas; schools like Berbice High, Tagore High, Corentyne High, R.N. High and Farley High to mention some of the more vibrant schools around. Thus, students, looking for an ideal opportunity, found refuge at Rose Hall High School. Because of this great surge, we had to build an additional smaller wooden building next to the existing structure of our main building. In the meantime, Rose Hall High School was becoming more and more successful and very well known. Our school was seen as a bright light of education in this Corentyne area, and this brought a great sense of pride and joy to us all. We were happy to see that our school was serving the needs of the children while serving the community.

The most amazing thing we saw was that Rudra was always encouraging, supporting, and promoting our students and teachers. He advocated that the teachers should always have our school at heart – to be good examples, to foster the interests of the students and to guide them towards higher goals and achievements. He wanted them to show the principle of integrity and respectability. Always, whenever there were problems with the teachers or students, he tried to resolve such with every care and concern seasoned with the salt of wisdom. Of course, this did not always work out as hoped.

After our transition, our students and teachers found a sense of harmony. We were seeing the enthusiasm for learning among our students and the dedication to teaching on the part of our teachers. We were feeling the wave of progress enveloping us and an educational surge moving through us. Efforts were now centered on gearing our senior students—the class of 1962—to sit for the Senior Cambridge Exam.

This Exam was administered by the Cambridge University in England and was designed for academically ambitious high school students. Certificates were awarded on the basis of a group of subjects passed. Those candidates who failed one paper in this group did not receive certificates. Those who passed had a great chance of finding employment in the Government or the private sectors of the workforce.

To meet the challenges of this Exam great emphasis was placed on students' learning and teachers' teaching. It seemed that the compasses of our minds were directed solely on passing this Exam.

Our anticipation for the results was very high. We were also aware that our competitive high schools in the area were waiting to see how we would match up with their results. Surprisingly, the results came and Rose Hall High School transcended our highest expectations. We never anticipated such outstanding results from our first batch of seniors, but we were exceedingly gratified with our results and to have had so many graduates. In fact, immediately following the results, the Principal of Corentyne High School, Mr. Chandi Singh, sent us a message congratulating our school for our fine achievement at the Exam. Besides, our Principal, Rudra Nath, did not hesitate to recruit our top graduates, and added them to our teaching staff. The other graduates went on to find gainful employment in the government or private sectors in our community or other parts of the country.

While all these remarkable undertakings were going on Rudra decided to incorporate the school and brought into the scene the

Board of Trustees (Governors). These members were recruited from the community. For a short while things went well. Then, problems about policies, financing and administration came into play. Obviously, the trust factor was in question. In the meantime, we were still going around collecting money from people in other areas not yet visited, and still we were entertaining the audience through concerts and continuing to promote education for our young children.

Matters between Rudra and the Board of Governors got worse. Their disputes, although the welfare of the students and teachers and even the community were at stake, could not find a resolution. There were many attempts at mediations between Rudra and the Board of Governors to find a reasonable compromise or solution but, there was none. Strangely enough, since the fate of the institution was at stake one would think there would be a compromise or improvement in the relationship between Rudra and the Board of Governors instead of allowing the institution to fall. But, there was none. It was during this time the teachers and the students decided to show their solidarity of support against the Board of Governors. The students, in particular, decided to stage a strike in strong protest against the Board of Governors. The students and teachers continued to be supportive of their principal, Rudra, in all these struggles. This rift between Rudra and the Board of Governors continued and matters got worse. In the meanwhile, teaching and learning were the activities of the day. While these problems were going on, our students were being prepared to write their up-coming Exam.

Day of the Strike - Student Council

ABOUT 400 STUDENTS GATHERED TOGETHER TO
PROTEST AGAINST THE BOARD OF GOVERNORS IN SUPPORT
OF RUDRA NATH

The following year (1962-1963) our students took the General
Certificate of Examination, 'O' level, administered by the University
of London, England. This Exam was more desirable because it could
be used by its graduates to gain admittance to higher institutions of
learning as well as employment purposes. This Exam was different
from the Senior Cambridge Exam in that a candidate did not have to
pass all subjects in a group to get a certificate.

We were more than determined to supersede the previous year
Exam results. The students were prepared to give it their all, and
the teachers were likewise giving them all the help they needed.
Encouragement, on the part of the teachers and dedication to studies
on the part of the students, were at a fever pitch high. Besides, there
was always competition among the students themselves.

Our students went and wrote the Exam and from their feedback the impression was they did very well. Finally, the results came. Again, the Exam results were beyond our expectations... they were fantastic! We could not believe the many students who graduated with high honors. Our school again was flying its #1 banner of high achievement high above the rest of the other high schools in the areas. Because of our great results, RHS was once again seen as the number one high school in the Corentyne area. After graduation, as expected, some of our students went on to higher education at the University of Guyana or abroad, while some entered the workforce. As for those who did not make it at the Exam they decided to give it another try. It must be noted that many of our GCE recipients after receiving their degrees studied on their own and wrote the GCE Advanced levels and were successful in several subjects indicating the high level of education received from our institution.

Our school was still confronted with the problems between Rudra and the Board of Governors. We were still hoping for the best. We were still doing our fund raising campaigns through our usual visitations --going from house–to-house, and doing our popular concert tours. Our numbers continued to grow. However, it seemed that we were all going through some kind of emotional, psychological as well as physical stress and this was affecting us. As to how much, we would never know. So, if you see any strange, unnatural behavior with any of us, don't be surprised; you know the cause—it was those darn Board of Governors. However, we still continued to prepare our students for the up-coming exam but the climate was different. As the case with Rudra and the Board of Governors continue to play out more drastically, this was having an even more negative impact on the whole school. Despite all the setbacks we faced our students of the 1963-1964 class went on to write the General Certificate of Examination, 'O' level.

The dark cloud of anxiety and despair loomed over us as tensions between Rudra and the Board of Governors continued. Their disputes had to be resolved in court at Georgetown, the capital. Rudra fought his battle valiantly but without a lawyer. He argued his case admirably but lacked supportive data especially his financial documentation. Consequently, he lost the case. The court placed an injunction on him depriving him to enter the school.

The teachers, students, and the community, however, stood by Rudra. They were there with him from the onset of the school; they believed that whatever money was collected by Rudra and his group of faithful teachers, students and key members of the community who were also his dear friends, was spent towards construction, paying teachers' salaries, scholarships and other costs relating to the maintenance and other pertinent expenses of the school. The only problem seen against Rudra was that he did not have a good accounting system - one that shows the income and the expenses of the school.

RUDRA SPEAKS TO PARENTS AND STUDENTS AT RHS ON THE LAST DAY. THE NEXT DAY RHS MOVES TO THE PORT MOURANT RACE COURSE PAVILLIONS.

(COURTESY OF VINCE RAMCHARRAN)

The court had ruled that Rudra could not enter RHS building, and an injunction was placed on him preventing him from doing so. Surprisingly, the police were there to enforce the law, making sure he could not enter the building. As a result of this, the entire school--students and teachers (a total of about 800 students and 30 teachers),--decided to follow Rudra to Port Mourant, where through the instrumentality of Mr. Rahaman it was arranged that RHS could use the Port Mourant Race Course Pavilion as their new location for their school.

THIS IS THE PORT MOURANT RACE COURSE WHICH TEMPORARILY HOUSED THE STUDENT AND TEACHERS (ABOUT 800 AND MORE) WHO WERE FORCED TO LEAVE RHS AT THE REEF (SWAMP) LOCATION.

CHAPTER 4

ROSE HALL HIGH SCHOOL FURTHER MOVE TO THE PORT MOURANT RACE COURSE

It seemed strange that no attempts were made by Rudra, nor by any legal group of concerned citizens, to awaken interests in the closed Rose Hall High School. When we think of all the enormous and committed sacrifice, we, the students, the teachers, and the community made to bring RHS at the "swamp" into existence and then to see how all our dreams were shattered, we feel an agony of utter loss, like the death of a dear friend; a pain that cannot be expressed. Why did all this have to happen?

However, time sometimes brings answers. It happened that years later a few of the Board of Governors did confess to a few of our faithful members who had taken an active part in the history of our schools, and to some of our teachers, that during the time when Rudra and the Board of Governors had problems about policy, finance, and administration about the school, that the Board of Governors did not treat Rudra fairly and that they acted that way because of the other members of the Board of Governors who were totally against the policies of Rudra. Also, one Board Member, whose brother was a teacher at RHS and who was with Rudra in all phases of RHS's undertakings (campaigns, money collections, and the expenditure of funds) stated that the Board of Governors gave Rudra an unfair, unjustified treatment which he did not deserve. Consequently, he resigned as member of the Board of Governors and instead, hooted for the cause of Rudra and RHS. But, could there be any comfort to resurrect this lost hope, the shattered dreams, the agonizing pains of a total loss for the children and teachers and parents and the community that gave their all to their beloved school, RHS?

We all had paid a great price! Nevertheless, the best news is our school was taken over by the Guyana government, and our beloved school was established as a free secondary high school.

We had to move on. It seemed strange that we were yet to build our Rose Hall High School all over again; this time at the Port Mourant Race Course Pavillion. This scene was already played out at the original Rose Hall High School when we converted the Rock Diamond Hotel entertainment center at the initial Rose Hall High School. Here, funds again were the problem.

RUDRA WITH TWO FRIENDS WITH HIS VOLKSWAGON. THIS CAR WAS RAFFLED AND THE FUNDS WENT TO HELP FINANCE THE SCHOOL (RHS). AT THE PORT MOURANT RACE COURSE PAVILLION. (VINCE RAMCHARRAN)

Rudra decided to raffle his car (his Volkswagon). With the money he received he bought essential requirements to give the school a jumpstart, like office supplies, chalk, blackboards, partition, and a host of other requirements. Obviously, teachers had to be paid. Soon, we were again ready to turn the wheel of time and move forward. Our classrooms, in a different environment, were all set to go. We stayed here for a short period of time. We were new to this environment. The racetrack was before us and in this open space were goats, cows, and donkeys grazing - seemingly, a pleasure to watch out in the open and enjoy the natural beauty that was before us. There was always something out there that attracted our students and teachers. Sometimes, though, the braying of the stallions would rent the air. This was usually, distracting; but we adjusted to our new environment. We were always making adjustments. Besides, this was a period of heavy rains, and it is said that when it rains it pours. The heavy rains brought about an infestation of mosquitoes and this was another major factor with which we had to deal. Also, there was no partition between classrooms and usually the noises were distracting. The fact is, most of these features were there when we got there and during our stay there we got accustomed to them - an inseparable part of the environment. At first, we were somewhat uncomfortable because we never faced these prevailing activities before, but soon we were becoming a part of it.

During this time, our GCE 'O' level results were in. Again, we expected good results despite the adverse setbacks we had to face. Surprisingly, the results transcended our highest expectations. We were overjoyed that our students went through so much under the struggles facing our school and that they were able to surmount those problems and to achieve such outstanding results. The results were exceptional! Our graduates again brought great honor to our institution with their high grades. We were again flying our number one banner high above the other high schools in the area. What a grand achievement and a laudable performance at a time when the pains of leaving our beloved RHS were still eating at the core of our being!

While all this was happening, Rudra was feverishly negotiating to move us to another place. We were, however, not very optimistic, but we kept the faith, believing that better times were coming. We were surprised, however, to learn that Rose Hall High School was to merge with Port Mourant Comprehensive Institute. This brought a cheerful and delightful satisfaction to our hearts. This also brought to light another episode in the history of Rose Hall High School.

It was no wonder that Rudra was trying so hard to move us to a better place. He always wanted what would be best for us. He envisioned that the August races were only about a month away and one can imagine the changes our school would have to make in order to accommodate the up-coming races. This meant we had to find another place to store all of our school equipments, materials and other supplies related to our school just to make room for the coming races. Then after the races we would have to readjust to our original classroom format. However, this move to merge with Port Mourant Comprehensive Institute was definitely approved. This name was later changed after the merger to Corentyne Comprehensive High School (CCHS). In light of all this, we were more than ready to join in the fun and enjoyment with the celebrants coming to the races. Why not? We too deserved to have a good time.

ANOTHER VIEW OF PORT

MOURANT RACE COURSE PAVILLION

THE TRACK AT PORT MOURANT RACE COURSE
WHICH COMES ALIVE IN THE MONTH OF AUGUST (THE
FIRST WEEK). NOTE THE STABLES ON THE LEFT AND THE
PAVILLION ON THE RIGHT.

THE AUGUST RACE AT PORT MOURANT RACE COURSE

During this time of the year coming close to the month of August, the sugar factories were closed for a short period of time, during which repairs, cleaning and general maintenance to the factories and their equipments were being done. It was at this time that the staff members and the executive members of the estates and their families with their elite friends, as well as special guests, would attend the Race Course and witness or participate in the races. The community also joyously participated.

Races were held the first week of August usually on a Saturday and on a Monday. The Port Mourant Race Course was the finest, largest, and most spectacular of the race tracks in the country — second only to Durban Park Race Course in Georgetown, our Capital. People would come from all over the Corentyne are: Port Mourant, Albion, Fyrish, Skeldon, and from New Amsterdam; even from Georgetown. It was not surprising to find people from other countries, (Trinidad and Surinam) who joined in the celebration, as well. The events and activities were so well designed that it seemed to have something for everybody; so everybody wanted to get into the action. People would arrive by whatever means possible: trucks, cars, buses, tractors with trailers, bicycles, only to participate in this grand and celebrated event. Along the public road and in the compound of the Race Course, vendors would try to select their best 'business' spots and display their merchandise: various articles, varieties of clothing, and food items. There were various assortments of drinks (sodas, liquor, beer, mauby, ginger beer, a special orange juice from Trinidad called, 'chowtal', and lots more. Then there were the attractive enticing games of dice; 'the three card game' and 'roll-a- penny and win a dollar' game, plus several other local games.

The coming of visitors, friends, families, children, vendors, workers, police, and others would create a crowded, busy, yet, a seemingly safe environment. The air is usually filled with a happy, jubilant sound with everybody seemingly having a good time. Yes, they were there to have a good time – eating, drinking, shopping and having fun – while meeting families, friends, or just wandering around sight- seeing.

The horse and the mule races were the main features of the day. Horses and mules came from several sugar estates from around the areas. There was sharp competition among these sugar estates — especially, Port Mourant and Pln. Albion. Mr. Rahaman, for instance, had his own horse stables. At one time, he had eight horses.

Many of these owners took part in the horse-racing events. Many other participants who were private owners also owned horses of their own and they too joined in the races. This was a place of great attraction and excitement. At one time, Queen Elizabeth and Prince Charles came to Port Mourant in their private helicopter. There was a grand celebration for them at the Race Course. This obviously was a very auspicious moment and it stirred quite an attraction.

Horse Racing was big business for the spectators and organizers. Some of the more popular horses were June Flower, Cracker Jack, Double Penny and Bright Steel to mention a few, while some of the top contenders among the mules were Venus, Herod, Zeus, and Zaya. In addition to big betting on the horse and mule racing, there were also other gambling activities.

Races usually start at one o'clock in the afternoon. There were only horse racing and mule racing events. Announcements would be made as to what race would begin and some general information about the race given. In the meantime, people would be purchasing tickets for a particular race. The races would then begin and this would be monitored with the final winner declared. The winners, of course, would collect on their winning tickets. Following this, the people would again move freely in the open compound until the beginning of the next race.

These events were very organized and police were patrolling as usual, watching out for problems. This movement would go on until 5 PM in the evening. Day two seem to run the same way with anticipation and excitement and in this way this episode with all the seeming pomp and glory would be brought to a close and expectations would be built again for the up-coming year. As for us we were ready to embark on a continued journey of our education – joining the Port Mourant Comprehensive Institute.

FROM PORT MOURANT RACE COURSE FOLLOWING THE MERGER, ROSE HALL HIGHSCHOOL MOVED TO PORT MOURANT COMPREHENSIVE INSTITUTE. THE NAME WAS CHANGED TO CORENTYNE COMPREHENSIVE HIGH SCHOOL..

CHAPTER 5

MERGER OF ROSE HALL HIGH SCHOOL (RHS) AND PORT MOURANT COMPREHENSIVE INSTITUTE (PMCI) TO CORENTYNE COMPREHENSIVE HIGH SCHOOL (CCHS)

Just as Rudra was the architect and pioneer in bringing Rose Hall High School into existence and helped establish it, John Muria was the other pioneer with a prophetic insight. He was instrumental in bringing Port Mourant Comprehensive Institute into existence. Iswar Prashad, a young, talented and ambitious Educator was selected as the principal. He was encircled with a group of faithful teachers, a new recruit of 30 students, and an indispensable secretary, Elaine Mallay. Under Prashad, Port Mourant Comprehensive Institute started to climb the ladder of success almost immediately, despite some of the problems this new school faced.

THE PREVIOUS BUILDING WAS MODIFIED TO WHAT IT IS TODAY.

Rose Hall High School (RHS) joined Port Mourant Comprehensive Institute (PMCI) to become Corentyne Comprehensive High School (CCHS) towards the end of 1964, with our student body risen to over 1000 students and about 35 teachers. Rudra, per contractual agreement, took over as principal with Ishwar Prashad and Vernon Asregadoo as assistant principals.

Here, we saw two different and unique institutions merged into one establishment incorporating different ideologies and philosophies. This union was not easy. There were many adjustments and flexibilities but we were able to see these two streams of institutions finding a confluence of a wonderful integration – no more a separate unity but a unified mix. The teachers and students of both schools found themselves wonderfully integrated and went on to establish a common goal and purpose – to be only the best.

Rudra stayed until the end of 1965. During his administration, the weight of responsibilities was overwhelming. It was as if starting anew, with new students, which never seem to stop coming. Rudra was always thinking of the students. He had planned to extend the activities of fund-raising among concerned citizens—well-wishers, wealthy businessmen and the like as well as through concerts and other fund-raising events etc. With the money thus acquired he had hoped to buy a few buses to facilitate the transportation of our students from distant areas to come to school in the morning and to transport them back at the end of the day. He had also planned to provide free lunches to needy kids—a real dire need—but this never materialized. He could not get the approvals as required. This did hurt him very much and obviously the kids too.

Our school under Rudra did not fail to implement as well as reinforce hard work, dedication and commitment among our teachers as well as among the students. He always made sure that respectability and moral character, coupled with discipline, were upheld.

CCHS was becoming quite an institution. It was even considered unparalleled in the area of education. In the sports arena we were always unmatched. Our cricket team caused quite a stir. We were always the number one cricket team in the area. It is no wonder we were labeled, 'the winning school for sports.' CCHS was also champion in the fields of volleyball, table tennis, and in the area of debates. In 1968 -1969, we were the regional champs for debates.

In 1965, our school was saddened to see our dear Rudra leave CCHS. He went on to found the National High School, which also became another success story. Rudra wore many hats – pioneer, principal, teacher and friend, and many other titles. His name will echo in the annals of our history for all services rendered in the pursuit and achievement of education for our children.

In 1966, Walter Ramdeholl was appointed as principal of Corentyne Comprehensive High School. He was the right choice for this outstanding office. He was very qualified with a BSc. Degree in Economics from London. He was not only a seasoned teacher but an administrator with outstanding credentials. Walter inherited a wonderful student body eager to learn, to make every sacrifice, and to achieve the ultimate. He also was blessed with a dedicated and hard-working staff. Walter knew what to do and how to do it. Immediately, he rallied his staff, tapping especially on Ishwar Prashad and Vernon Asregadoo and his faithful, competent, and trustworthy teachers. He was able to implement his best strategies and resourcefulness, to raise the standard of education even more. In 1967, our students from CCHS at the GCE 'O' level Exam, unleashed their scholastic capabilities with the outcome that great outstanding achievements were still being achieved. Our school's banner as number one in academics was again flying high.

Our school continued to do very well through the years under Walter Ramdeholl. I left CCHS in March of 1970 to pursue higher studies abroad. However, there were many other changes that occurred in the passage of time until the Guyana government negotiated a takeover making CCHS a Government Entity, which eventually provided free education for all high school students in the area.

CHAPTER 6

STUDENTS AND TEACHERS ARE HONORED FOR MENTORSHIP AND SCHOLASTIC ACHIEVEMENTS......AND A POEM

TO: THE STUDENTS OF RHS, PMCI AND CCHS

I, Adarsh Hari, would like to take this opportunity to honor each of you, my dear former students, in your great journey through the corridors of RHS, PMCI and CCHS. You, as students have come from different and varied backgrounds of life. You had made the unimaginable sacrifices, the worthwhile and dedicated efforts only to focus on this most challenging undertaking – to get an education with help coming from your parents and others. You came to realize and you decided to give it all you got.

Only you can testify and fathom the struggles and hardships you went through for so many years. Even when chores at home were demanding and your financial situation may not have been the best, you focused on your lessons at school. This was not easy but you did not give up. Even when there were problems with the school and its transitions, when our journey was bleak and uncertain, you stood strong and tall and you did not give up. You put your hands to the plow and there was no turning back. Amidst these turbulent times you were resolute, unflinching and you never gave up. You held on to your ideals and your convictions to the very end.

In all your efforts, through your struggles and sacrifices, you were faithful. You knew you were making a genuine commitment to ensure a prospective future. You knew that making workable plans today was a sure investment for tomorrow's security. You made a total sacrifice to pursue your dream – your education…. and you achieved it.

To you, my dear friends, my sincerest congratulations! Thank you,

TO THE TEACHERS OF RHS, PMCI AND CCHS

To you, my fellow teachers, who have labored through all the ordeals and struggles and through the diverse episodes in the history of RHS, PMCI and CCHS, yours was a labor of love. Although you were not paid enough, as it were, you went above and beyond the call of duty and expectations. You were relentless in your pursuit to serve and ever attempting to bring success to our students. You were a model and you were expected to set a good example, and you did, although you were as old as some of the students themselves.

Your whole range of efforts was to motivate the students not only to help them pass the College of Preceptors, nor the Senior Cambridge nor even the GCE 'O' Level Exam, but to be a good and worthy human being -- noble and successful.

Many of you had to teach more than one subject, but you never complained. You were there to give your best only to make the students better. You were their guide, teacher, counselor, friend, and a parent, among other roles. You were always looking out for their interests, first and foremost.

For all your dedication, hard work and patience, and your struggles through it all, you inspired hope and faith in these students and motivated them in their aspirations to succeed. Yes, each of you have helped create and certainly helped to establish a great foundation for our students and in this lies our deepest joy and our grandest satisfaction and achievement. You, my fellow teachers, you have given your lifeblood in helping the students work towards their goal, aspiration and their establishment. To each of you, I extend my special congratulations!

A POEM BY ADARSH KUMAR HARI

Yes, my dear former students and my dear fellow teachers, you have waded the waters of Education and struggled against its relentless tides and have constantly looked at the beacon of hope ever striving onwards and upwards. Eventually, you have reached a comforting arena of satisfaction. You are able to find solace, and comfort, and eventually success in this your adventure. Because education has been our goal, our foundation, and its longing pursuit, and because its perimeters keep on shifting and changing, we constantly need to be reinforced with the required resources to meet its changing and challenging demands. In this pursuit you have all labored towards Education and to all of you I would like to dedicate the following poem: "MAMA, PLEASE, I WANNA LEARN."

It captures some of the measures and expectations we all had to face, yet, it inspires us with aspirations to climb the never-ending reaches of success.

"Mama I wanna learn all about me, who I am and what I can really be;

I wanna learn about my family too, 'cause I am part of my family tree.

I wanna learn about the schools' three R's and other concepts of life's education

I wanna learn like others before me and add to this quest my contribution.

I wanna learn all about my country: the people, the government and this great land;

I wanna learn about this noble nation, and the wonderful things that make her grand.

I wanna learn about other nations too; the important roles, they, in history played

I wanna learn what makes them different and how each nation is uniquely made.

I wanna learn about this universe too, and how this creation came to be.

I wanna learn about the Creator too whose existence seems a mystery.

Mama, I wanna learn many things more, too numerous now for me to say.

These things will be part of my life's drama. Please Mama, I wanna learn it all, I pray.

CHAPTER 7

NARRATIVES BY STUDENTS AND TEACHERS CONCERNING THEIR ACADEMIC JOURNEYS

JOURNEY FOLLOWED BY A POEM

We are so proud to have the narratives of some of our former students and teachers who have journeyed the halls of learning at RHS, PMCI and CCHS. In their narration they have revealed their unique experiences, their cherished hopes and memories that are so much a part of their scholastic life in their pursuit towards education. We are also able to see who these achievers are as they reveal themselves. Through the education acquired and their determination and dedication to be better, they have certainly built a strong foundation for themselves that enabled them to gain greater successes through life's meandering corridors.

Garnered from the annals of the past, we cherish the opportunities given us by those who extended their hands and touched us. They have made a difference in our lives. To the hands that touched us, we acknowledge and give honor.

Here is a poem that expresses the sentiments of those that have been blessed and who remember the magic touch of those hands as they travel life's journey.

"SOMEONE STRETCHED OUT A HAND AND TOUCHED ME."BY ADARSH HARI

Sweet Joy fills my heart like never before,

And love seems to flow from an open door,

My whole world lights up like bulbs on a tree,

'Cause someone stretched out a hand and touched me.

My mind soars high on the loftiest mount,

And my being draws love from Life's pure fount.

My thoughts are filled with entrancing beauty,

'Cause someone stretched out a hand and touched me.

I don't know why I am feeling like this;

I may call it ecstasy or maybe bliss.

Life's wondrous ways I'm beginning to see,

'Cause someone stretched out a hand and touched me

I now behold a purpose for living.

I want to share in the love of giving

New meanings to life I now come to see

'Cause someone stretched out a hand and touched me.

Here are some of those who have stretched out their hands and touched us at RHS, PMCI and CCHS. Many of them have passed away but their unique legacy, dedication and service will still echo in our hearts.

HERE IS A LIST OF THOSE PROFESSIONALS: PRINCIPALS, ASSISTANT PRINCIPALS, TEACHERS AND OTHERS:

Asregadoo Vernon, (Assistant Principal, RHS & CCHS). Bacchus Azim, Banergie Jack, Bhajan Deonarine, Bhajan Norma, Birbahadur Mohanlall, Boodram Dennis, Doobay Krishna, Etwaroo Leslie, Hari Adarsh, Haripersaud 'Brazo', Joseph Ralph, Kempadoo Gilford, Kewalall Lakraj, Lall Soman, Latcha Milton, Latchana Tai, Madho Chandradutt, Miser Amrita, Nagamootoo Moses, Naidoo Kenneth, Narine Chandradutt, Nath Rudra, (Principal for RHS and CCHS), Nathoo Julius, Permaul James, Persaud Kessoo, Persaud Sarju , Peters Samuel, Prashad Ishwar (Principal, PMCI; Assistant Principal, CCHS), Punwassie Hardutt, Sanichar Sagar, Rai Kamal Ramsagar, Walter Ramdeholl, (Principal, CCHS), Ramkeerat Subas, Ramkissoon Chunilall, Ramnarine Gajraj, Rawana William, Roopan Mahendranath, Sankar Yassin, Sharma Deodat , Shrinarine Doromattie, Seecharran Jai, Singh Chatterpaul, Singh Julip, Singh Raymond, Singh Stanley Latchman, Sukra Prema, Surujpaul, Jatischand (Cats), Yassim Haman Ben.

RUDRA WITH HIS 18 TEACHERS AT ROSE HALL HIGH
SCHOOL AT THE REEF (SWAMP)

Front row (left to right): Hardat Punwassie, deonarine Bhajan, Sagar Sanichar, Basil Jaggernath, Kenneth Naidoo.

Second row: L to R: Hamman Yassim, Surujpaul (Cats), Jatischand, Dharo Shrinarine, Hanna Prema, Narine Chando, Brazo Haripersaud, Subas Ramkerat, William Rawana, Stanley LAtchman Singh, Rudra Nath.

Last row: L to R: Adarsh Hari, Gajraj Ramnarine, Mohanlall Birbahadur and Tai Lachana

Other Professionals: Elaine Mallay, Rita Butcher (Secretaries), Surinarain Abo (Managing the canteen) and the Watchman and Caretaker, James Austin.

ANOTHER GROUP F STUDENTS SHOWING THEIR
UNIOQUE UNIFORMS WITH BOOKS IN HANDS AND
REFLECTING AN AIR OF HIGH SCHOOL PRIDE (COURTESY
OF ROOPDAI GOPAUL)

HERE ARE THE NARRATIVES AND PICTURES OF THE STUDENTS AND TEACHERS WHO WOULD HAVE THOUGHT

BY ERROL ARTHUR

During her senior year at University in Philadelphia, Pennsylvania my daughter called to inform me that she was skipping classes for a week to travel to Fort Benning, Georgia to protest against the Western Hemisphere Institute for Security Cooperation (formerly the School for the Americas). This is a military training school for Latin American and Caribbean soldiers and has been described in many circles as the biggest base for destabilization in the region. My fatherly protective instincts immediately kicked in as I voiced my concerns about her safety as well as ramifications for her future that, in her youthful exuberance and idealism, she might not have taken into consideration. Where did this come from, I wanted to know. She responded with ill-disguised glee that she had inherited it from me, the very man who was now displaying the unmitigated gall to voice concerns about her activism.

But, I had never discussed my own activism with her, nor did I ever encourage her to do likewise. She taught me a valuable lesson in leadership by example that day. For the first time I looked inward and tried to understand what she was forcing me to confront. And then it hit me. The culprit was Rudra Nath and Rose Hall and Corentyne Comprehensive High Schools (RHS/CCHS). They provided me an education that went well beyond the three R's. The conjugation of verbs and trigonometry were important, but so was the mandate that I was my brother's keeper. No classes were ever held on this, just leadership by example.

One manifestation of this was the issue of lavatory facilities for the school. After four years of existence and eight hundred students, RHS still had pit latrines. When the wind was not cooperative, concentration on Shakespeare, the rules for the sequence of tenses, and quadratic equations became quite difficult. The Board of Governors, to whom he had magnanimously ceded control of the school, adamantly refused his request to fund the building of proper lavatories. Too expensive, they argued. For Rudra this was intolerable, and never one to allow the myopia of others to subvert his vision, he chose the route of rebellion and action.

He assembled some of the faithful - students, teachers, and parents - and laid out the following scenario. He was going to use the money he collected from tuition fees to purchase the building supplies for the construction of the lavatories and have them delivered on a Friday afternoon after the Law Courts had closed. He was positive that the Board would be first in line when the Courts opened on Monday morning to charge him with embezzlement of funds (the unauthorized expenditure of tuition fees) and to issue an injunction on him to stop work on the project. It was imperative, therefore, that the project (from excavating for the septic tank, to laying concrete, to plumbing, etc.) be completed by midday Monday before the marshals came either to arrest him or to serve the injunction, or both. He knew that he was going to be fired and dragged before the courts. He might lose the school which he founded and had given his lifeblood to sustain. But, he argued, eight hundred students would never again have to use pit latrines. The lavatories were built, the marshals came, Rudra was fired, and he lost the school.

But did that derail his mission? Absolutely not! The entire school abandoned the edifice they had themselves constructed and moved to the Port Mourant Race Course to hold classes. It was a show of defiance and solidarity that was fabulous and inspiring to behold. Shortly thereafter Rose Hall High School merged with the Port Mourant Comprehensive Institute and the Corentyne Comprehensive High School was born. Leadership by example!

I shudder to think about what would have become of me, my sister, Millicent and brothers, Stephen, Leon and Lennox were we denied the secondary education that Guyanese now take for granted. We were raised by a single mother who earned a meager salary as a public servant at the Port Mourant Hospital. But, she had great dreams for her seven children – dreams of opportunities that she never had, and which could not have been realized if those pioneers, Rudra Nath, Adarsh Kumar Hari, Udai Panday, and John Muria did not have the vision to conceive what they did, and the courage and forbearance to implement it. Founding RHS/CCHS were not exercises in entrepreneurship as it was to satisfy a crying need – the need to provide the only passport out of the poverty and hopelessness to which we were all condemned.

I do not measure my individual life's journey through my personal achievements, although they do give me great satisfaction. I am eminently proud of that poor country boy who was condemned by accidents of history, geography, and birth to a life of unrealized potential who rose to the ranks of senior management in the government in Washington, DC. None of that would have been possible if Rose Hall High School did not accept me into its fold even though I did not meet the age and income qualifications demanded by other high schools in the country, and educate me out of the poverty and helplessness that seemed my fate. My story is not unique. All those who have passed through those doors have their own stories to tell – stories that begin with pessimism, hopelessness and despair and end with optimism, achievement, hope, success, and courage – all against seemingly insurmountable odds.

But, I take greater pride and satisfaction in achievements in the promotion of freedom and social justice, however modest may have been my contribution, in which I have been engaged. That is what I cherish the most from my RHS/CCHS experience. Rudra and his staff taught me by example not to curse the darkness but to light a candle. Now my own daughter has told me that, without saying a word, I have imbued the same in her. Yes, indeed, I have come a far way.

HERE ARE THE NARRATIVES AND PICTURES OF THE STUDENTS AND TEACHERS Manilla Asregadoo

Before After

MY ACADEMIC JOURNEY AND SIGNIFICANT EXPERIENCES AT ROSE HALL HIGH SCHOOL AND AFTER

Your school years can have a significant impact on the path you take in life. My name is Manilla Asregadoo nee Lackraj-Anjan and I grew up in Williamsburg, Corentyne, Berbice. It was an honor to be asked by Mr. Hari, a former Rose Hall High School teacher, to share my experience at Rose Hall High School and its impact on my educational journey. I attended Rose Hall High School for a year and during my attendance there I learned about the struggle and sacrifice made by fellow students for higher education. I learned to be persistent and also I learned about the importance of cooperation.

In January 1961, thanks to Mr. Rudra Nath, the principal, I was admitted to Rose Hall High School. I had already attained "School Leaving Certificate," The Pupil Teachers' Appointment Certificate" and "The College of Preceptors' Certificate." However, I needed to obtain the "Senior Cambridge Certificate." Under the tutelage of instructors, Julius Nathoo, Vernon Asregadoo and H. Yassim, I received the "Senior Cambridge Certificate" in December of 1961.

One of the things that stood out most vividly, in my memory, was the co-operation between teachers, students, and the community in their effort to build the school. The school had overcrowded classes and there was an effort to expand the school. Therefore, there were many areas under construction to extend and accommodate more classes. It still amazed me that so many students and teachers volunteered to stay after school to help with the construction of classroom. They mixed the cement and helped to build the concrete walls.

Concerts and other fund raisers were held to raise money to build the structure at the "Reef Section" down Market Street at Rose Hall Village. At that time, Corentyne High School was the only established High School in the Lower Corentyne area. However, the advent of Rose Hall High afforded many students the opportunity of a higher education. Later, Rose Hall High School merged with Corentyne Comprehensive High School.

My experience at Rose Hall High School gave me the motivation to pursue higher education led me to write and pass The Advanced Level GCE in Geography. Soon after I taught at St. Joseph's Anglican School. Then in 1968, I was accepted in the In-Service Teachers' Training Program. I graduated with a Trained Teacher's Certificate in 1970. This was a great achievement and I have to thank my husband and my parents for their support and encouragement during that time as my daughter was just six months old when I started the course.

My teaching career took me to many schools in different parts of the country. I taught at New Market Anglican School when my husband was appointed Deputy Headmaster of that school, at St. John's Anglican school, Anna Catherina when my husband was appointed Headmaster at St. Jude's Anglican School at Blankenberg, West Demerara. I taught at Ascension Anglican School at Soesdyke East Bank, Demerara when my husband accepted the post as Headmaster of St. Mary's Anglican School.

On our return to Berbice, I taught at St. Joseph's Anglican School as my husband was appointed Headmaster of Albion Government School and later Headmaster of the Community High School at Port Mourant. It was daunting at first as I had to leave friends and relatives work and settle in new and unfamiliar locations. However, it turned out to be a great experience for me, moving to different areas of the country, meeting new people, making new friends and above all working with children from different socio - economic backgrounds. I taught for seventeen years in Guyana.

When I migrated to the USA, I inquired about teaching in the New York City Public School. However, I found that it was vastly different from that in Guyana. So I changed career! I began working for National Bank of America which later became National Westminster Bank. During the thirteen years that I worked in the banking industry, I was placed in seven different locations due to promotional opportunities.

I enrolled at York College, however, in my third year I decided to leave due to the long hours and responsibility of my job. Upon the insistence and encouragement of my husband and daughters, I returned to complete my Accounting degree. After graduating from college with a BSC degree in Accounting, I left my employment with the bank. I worked temporarily at Social Security Administration and subsequently worked for a year at the "Visa Section" of the Immigration and Naturalization Services at 26 Federal Plaza in Manhattan. I then, transferred to Social Security Administration in Queens. I worked there until I retired in June 30, 2010. My husband retired from Stanley Morgan Dean Witter Brokerage firm, which was located on Five World Trade Center, after the 9 /11 disaster.

The life lessons I learned at Rose Hall High School has helped me to persevere when things did not quite work out the way I wanted them to. I became determined to succeed. I remember the struggles of the students who dreamt of getting a good education and of everyone working together for a common cause! Even though, I attended this school for one year, I cannot forget the wonderful mentors who helped me to become the person I am today. I made wonderful friends, many of whom I am still in contact with. The experience at Rose Hall High School has left a lasting impression on my life!

V.E. Asregadoo, former Deputy Principal

1959- 1962

Rose Hall High School

It was September 1959, I moved from the Port Morant High School, the first such private school that catered for those whose sole ambition was to move from Primary school level to have a High School preparation, a level before College education. I then found myself with a group of young teachers led by a stranger in my community, Port Mourant, Corentyne, Berbice, Guyana.

I was offered the Deputy Principal position as I had had two years of teaching and administration previously. This new school was housed in a building that was once a Hotel where life was very different. Some of those who were guests there were also invariably known for indulging in not-so-aspiring goals- gambling and prostitution.

All of these adventures in life took place a year prior to the founding of Rose Hall High school where we were to educate youngsters in the Arts and Sciences.

This was a challenge as we had to build a High School climate in a society that already had an established High School - the Corentyne High School led by an ambitious teacher from Trinidad and Tobago.

My position was envied at first as some of the young teachers were there before me. I established a working rapport with the faculty and students.

I initiated an Evening school for adults who wanted to improve their education and set a role model for younger people in the society.

The years rolled by, and our staff and students proved to the society that we were there to stay and succeed alongside an established high school--the Corentyne High School.

The society soon saw evidence of excellent results at - the Senior Cambridge Exam, an examination run by Cambridge University in London, England. Rose Hall High School secured one Grade I, three Grade II's, and several Grade III's-- an achievement that startled the community. The Principal of the Corentyne High School sent a congratulatory message as he himself had felt Rose Hall High School would not survive.

The building where Rose Hall High School was housed soon became overcrowded and uncomfortable for the growing school population.

It was at this time that we involved the society in contributing to our new school building fund. The faculty and the Board of Trustees along with some students started planning a series if concerts, public meetings, and house - to - house units to inform the public of our intentions to construct a school building for our school. This fund-raising netted over $13,000.00.

After several months of hard work, both with the academics and the school- building project, we had to procure a plot of land in an area that was considered a swamp.

What a fantastic transformation! After several months of hard work by students, teachers, villagers, and a few paid carpenters, and a capable contractor from the board of Governors, the basis of this massive 120ft. X 33ft. concrete structure was laid.

Students and teachers were involved in making concrete blocks by the hundreds. The building was built and the students produced great results at the Senior Cambridge Examination, General Certificate of Education Examinations from London, England and from the College of Preceptors, England.

Success in both examinations and building structure satisfied the public. Rose Hall High School was now established and growing. The Ministry of Education congratulated the Board of Trustees on its success and contributions to education in the community.

It was now 1962, and I was asked by Mr. Rudra Nath, to help another community in a district called Mahaicony. I left Rose Hall High School to assume the position of principal at the Ashram High School in Mahaicony.I still kept in touch with Rose Hall High School which soon developed problems with the Board of Trustees. The school later merged with another school, the Corentyne Comprehensive High School, and found a new home there.

Eileen –Bhajan 1961 to 1964

Eileen Bhajan—Eileen Sookhoo--- Eileen Seecharran

 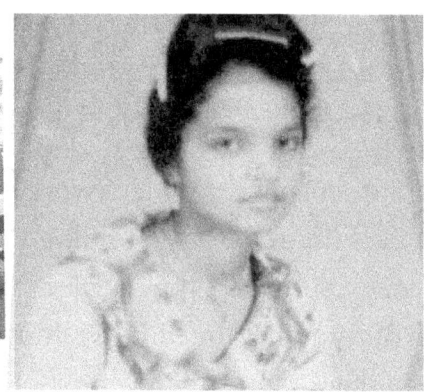

Before   After

These names refer to the same person. It is not a metamorphosis for I am no butterfly. It is just a biographic change. My father, William Bhajan was a resident of Rose Hall Town while my mother, Louisa Clarissa Nee Burgith, lived at Eversham Village. They are both deceased I am married to my fellow villager – Clement Seecharan. We are both the proud parents of Jennifer and Semone as well as the grandparents of two grandsons and four granddaughters.

I will endeavor to give my life story as it relates to my educational journey along the road to success. These experiences will reflect the good times and bad times throughout my early years.

Having completed primary school in 1959 I started classes at the commercial school in Rose Hall until 1960. In December I was at my Aunt's house when Mr. Rudra Nath was visiting my cousin, Esther, who was a student of Rose Hall High. He inquired who I was. He was told that my father died at age 37 leaving nine children to be taken care of by their 32 years old mother. Life was a struggle. It was difficult for her to supply us with food and clothes. She leaned on the everlasting arms of God. She was always praying for us and trusting Him to provide.

Mr.Nath, out of love and compassion, told my aunt to send me to RHS the next week. He offered me a scholarship. This was the greatest turning point in my life. I realized I had to work hard to justify his offer – that I was a suitable candidate as well as a deserving case.

From then onwards I started real diligent studies to keep my scholarship and to prepare myself for the ultimate goal – writing London G.C.E and Senior Cambridge Exams. I was promoted to form four from form two-- a feat that entailed hard work and performance. I even used waking tablets to help me from sleeping so that I could put in longer hours of study. One night I studied until 530 in the morning. I did not realize it was so late until I heard the neighbor's radio broadcasting the 'Indian Hour Program.'

Living conditions were poor at my aunt's house. I made my bed on the floor throughout my high school years. My mother could not afford new uniforms for me. Her alternative plan however, was to turn my green skirt inside out so that the outside looked new. Yes, I realize we were very poor and this fired up my ambition even more.

While others enjoy the luxury of new outfits, I was content with what I had. My friend, Somattie Ramtage, gave me bus fare to go home on Fridays and her mother made dresses for me. On Monday mornings I brought back with me items for my aunt – rice, vegetables, coconut oil and firewood instead of cash.

My high school life was interesting yet it was fraught with sacrifice. Through grit and determination, I successfully completed G.C.E and the Senior Cambridge Exams. As a result, I became qualified to teach and this brought me closer to achieving my lifelong ambition. I started out as a schoolteacher on May 12, 1964 at Yakusari Govt. School. Having spent three years there. I was transferred to Eversham Church Of Scotland School – next door to our house – the same school I attended as a pupil and here I taught for nearly 20 years. While I was there teaching I attended the teacher training in service – 1968 to 1970. As a teacher at Aversham Church of Scotland School I served in different capacities – assistant mistress, senior mistress and acting headmistress.

In 1986 Clement and I left Guyana for Tortolla British Virgin Islands where we continued our teaching career until 1989 when we emigrated to the USA. I left teaching and have been employed by the Alberta Manor, a Residential Home Care facility, for nearly 17 years. By virtue of my life's background and experiences I am able to make the lives of these residents more comfortable and meaningful.

Looking back. I feel I have had a full and happy life – one that afforded me great satisfaction, yet, helping me to provide quality service in my 25 years of teaching and years of service and care to the elderly and less fortunate. My success cannot be measured by the money I made but by the thousands of lives I have been able to touch. I remember, one of the beneficiaries during my teaching career at Eversham Primary School a former student, Keith Derrick Cummings, one who taught Neuro Science at St. George's Medical School in Canada and who now is a Medical Doctor at a hospital in Tuscaloosa, Alabama.

With a great sense of gratitude, I acknowledge contributions made by various people – teachers at Eversham Primary, Rose Hall

High and tutors of In-service Teachers Training College. It is the good Lord who has carried me through all my struggles and has blessed me so that I can serve others. I want to give a special thanks to my dear mother who has given me so much through her ultimate sacrifice. Glad that I was able to share my love with her and in my heart to share the sentiments with these words: "Mom, I love you".

Thank you Mr. Hari – A job well done. You inspired me. Your phone calls made a difference. It inspired me to write this episode. Yes, our journey has been long, but wonderful yet unforgettable. Glad I was a part of it. My sincere congratulations to all of you.

Finally, I say: Be humble, love one another, overcome evil with good. Our lives will soon pass away; make wise use of your time. Remember: today's a new day, yesterday is gone and tomorrow is not in our hands. So, be the best you can today.

RAHIM BAKSH

MY JOURNEY AT RHS

My name is Rahim Baksh and most of my friends at Rose Hall High School called me Baksh. I was born at plantation Port Mourant and I attended the St. Joseph Anglican school until the age old 12. Both my parents were plantation workers. After being so tired of working there, my parents decided to move a step further. We then moved away from the sugar estate and started a village life. I lived as a village rustic for approximately 9 years doing light farming and rice cultivation together with other minor household chores. I grew up with two sisters and three brothers. At that time my father was a peddler, and the sole support of the family. I lived a village rustic life for 10 years then one day I changed my mind after learning that a new high school will be opening at Rose Hall Village under the strict supervision of the well-known character by the name of Mr. Rudra Nath. I went to meet him and finalize my acceptance in the school.

On January 3, 1959 the school commenced and the students were pouring in great numbers. The students were separated in forms according to their academic level. I happened to join the third form due to some experiences I had at high school work. Unfortunately, I only spent two years at Rose Hall High School then I wrote the

College of Preceptors examination and I receive a passing grade. So did many of my other friends and colleagues. During that time the principal and the teachers were Rudra Nath, Adarsh Hari, Odai Panday, and Banergie. These teachers taught English, Latin, history, Math, Hindi and literature. Then subsequently, came Raymond Singh, and Vernon Asregadoo, who taught Math, Religious Kknowledge, and Geography.

Rose Hall High School was well organized under the leadership of Rudra Nath and his awesome staff of teachers. Our body of students continued to increase and soon it was time to move on to a bigger school. The school with the body of board of governors agreed to construct a new building at Rose Hall waterside, the school which I never attended. After my two years of Rose Hall High School, I was offered a job at the Black Bush Polder Rice and Land Development Scheme as a Ranger. During the process of my employment I usually visited the new school site at Rose Hall waterside.

I was very surprised to see so many of my friends and my Associates along with teachers and well-wishers helping in the project of building the school. I was so happy to see my best friends helping every weekend. Friends, like Nandlall Ramdhan and Soman Lall and others helping there also. My dear friend and trust- worthy brother, Jaisook Lakraj, was there with his family's tractor and trailer transporting dirt and sand for the landfill at the school. Since I did not spend any time in the development of the school site and as I did not attend that school I am unable to give my views but I know that the project was very successful.

Going to Rose Hall High School has changed me so much that I can now understand the realities of this life and the good things it brings to us a little bit more. The teachers were awesome, but Rudra Nath was phenomenal. May his soul rest in peace! For a short time,

I was in school Rudra Nath and I became close friends. Once he invited me to his home for lunch. He also trusted me with zeal and enthusiasm. He trusted me to develop the designs of the students' school ties which I made. I last met him in the US 10 years ago.

To all my friends and colleagues who are reading these words and find any mistakes or anything insultive, please forgive me. I like to express that it has been a great journey for me as I look back at my Rose Hall school days.

HIGH SCHOOL DAYS BY DENNIS BOODRAM

FORMER STUDENT, 1967-1962;

FORMER TEACHER, 1967-1970

IMAGINE it is graduation day. Everyone is happy and ready for a unique life experience. After all, "high school days" are over. The teachers are attired in academic gowns with square hats on their heads. The girls are beautifully dressed, elaborate make-up and the hair-do is upbeat! The guys are in tuxedos, young men ready to escort lovely young ladies. The photographers are ready. The valedictorian is set to deliver the main address. What a magnificent setting. There is magic in the air.

After graduation there is a grand party. The parents have left. They drove home. The students are going to a 5-star hotel to celebrate. These are young adults getting ready for colleges and universities. What a ball.!!! Just IMAGINE the fun, frolic and happiness, just IMAGINE. Yes, you can say "I'm a dreamer, but I'm not the only one"

You see in the 60's at the Corentyne Comprehensive High School, we were students of a different time and place. Academia and the affluence of society were not exactly intertwined. Yes, we had an institution called, "our high school". After so many years our teachers and fellow students immortalize the establishment, it is still "our high school" where we all long to return to the carefree days of the teenager-- hungry for love and learning the lessons of life.

My time as a student saw me through adolescence into a teenager. Learning the academic subjects and being taught by my teachers, my mentors, propelled me into an individual who wanted to compete and I immersed myself into a frenzy of learning. The attainment of GCE "0" levels and later "A" levels was the passport to indicate a higher level of education. That was the yardstick of measurement for success at that time. I do hope it has since changed.

Later on I was appointed to teach at the said school, "my high school", my alma mater. Learning from my now colleagues had never stopped. I was young and inexperienced. They were much more mature and became a superb "role model" to me. I was still being moulded by my teachers. How can one ever thank a teacher?

It reminds me of the song "To Sir with Love" from the movie of the said name- a true story inspired and experienced by a Guyanese teacher, E.R. Braithwaite, in England.

Whenever I think of the carefree, fun-loving and happy days, the high school years come to mind. Everyone will agree with me that these days went by fast, too fast. Looking back, the "DO" things at school were not all that bad. Wearing an identifiable uniform to distinguish us from students of other high schools was a good thing. We had our own identity. What about calling our teachers "Sir" and "Miss"? Respect, respect, respect was the order of the day. How about doing homework/assignments? We must have it ready for the next class, otherwise we have to fabricate some good excuses. However, not everything was generally acceptable as well.

Passing the prescribed GCE exams was the key to academic excellence. If a student did not pass, he/she was only passing through. Today such a perception is highly debatable and subjected to challenge. The academic high achievers were an upward sharp trajectory, the rest were simply non-achievers. This stigma to me did not lead to intellectual regeneration, except for a selected few.

The reunion at New York City in 2009, led me, as well as, many others to experience and embrace the success of an enduring community of students now men and women. Everyone I spoke to has done exceedingly well and excelled in their chosen career!!! High schools must be criticized for having unclear limits as to what signifies success for a student. I do hope that in contemporary education there is a restoration of institutional balance as to what student success really is. The curious contradiction as to what constituted student success could be argued that education was really the physiological and psychological maturation of the student and cultivating "the flexibility of the mind".

I would like to think that the education of today is to make the students curious, critical, and challenging in a climate where apathy often reigns. It is not to only pass the GCE exams. The sincere and heartfelt feelings which sometimes creep up on me whenever I think of high school days are not so much academic endeavours. Rather they are reminiscent of laughter, deeper and greater appreciation of the opposite sex-the hormones were on overdrive, fun times, and to grow emotionally and physically into adulthood. Yes, Economics, Mathematics and Literature were important, but the liberal approach to education is what takes precedence over time. (Emphasis mine)

As the autumn of our life approaches, somehow the things we have all experienced and learnt at high school-our formative years-will assist each and everyone of us to accept and face with dignity our declining years. It reminds me of a passage from the Bible, Ecclesiastes 3:1 "to everything there is a season, a time for every purpose under heaven." old days were the best days of my life. Just IMAGINE- "and they say I'm a dreamer, but I'm not the only one"----- John Lennon.

RAJGOPAUL AND RICKDAI CHUNILALL

I, was born at Port Mourant, Guyana, South America. I hail from a family of seven siblings, I being the eldest son. My father, a successful businessman at that time, had no desire for me to further my education, but to assist in his business. Had it not been for the opening of Rose Hall High School I would have been stuck with the family business. I remembered being at home for a year, helping in the shop when my neighbor and childhood friend, Isardat Ramdehol, told me that he was attending Rose Hall High School. That night I could not sleep and begged my parents to give me the opportunity to have a high school education.

I started Rose Hall high school in 1959 and was in Mr. Hari's Form 1 class. Mr. Hari taught Latin and Religious Knowledge. Mr. Pandey, Mathematics. Mr. Yassinm, Literature and Mr. Benargee, English. After one term a few of us were given accelerated promotions for hard work.

Studies at school and working in the shop after school were rough for me. Our shop would close at 10 PM and then my studies would start. I spoke with Mr. Nath about this. He was kind enough to visit my home and was able to convince my father to give me more time to study. For this, I am forever indebted to him.

Those years spent at Rose Hall High school were the best years of my life. It was a great learning experience. I was able to meet and bond with quite a number of friends: Ramnarace Karran, Lionel Jadoo, Mahendranath Budhar, Malahoo Basdeo, Rebecca Khanai, Basmattie Ramjeet and several others. Among our classmates there was genuine love and friendship and seemingly an eternal bond.

We studied hard; were eager to learn as we took our studies very seriously. We studied in groups and shared our textbooks and notes. We were given an all- round training –"to live and to live with". I and most of my classmates successfully wrote the College of Preceptors examination in 1961, the Senior Cambridge in 1962, and the London GCE (O) level in 1963. My last days at school were spent at the Rose Hall swamp area.

After graduating from high school I was appointed assistant master at Mibikuri school in 1963. Fourteen other graduates from Rose Hall High School were also appointed as teachers here. This surely marked an outstanding feature and achievement in the history of our school.

Although we were a young and inexperienced staff the training and inspiration we gained from Mr. Rudra Nath and his teachers helped us to excel not only in sports but also in education and an all round discipline along with the spirit of self-help to the community in which we lived. Here I met my wife Rickdai Singh. We were married in 1965 and have two sons who reside with their families in the USA and one daughter who resides with her family in Canada.

After graduating from the Teachers Training college IN-service, we were transferred to Tain Primary school, where both my wife and I taught at the common entrance classes for over 12 years. Later I was appointed Senior Master at Winifred Gaskin secondary school and Headmaster at Albion Primary. I retired in 1998. My wife was also appointed Senior Mistress at J.C. Chandisingh Secondary school and later Deputy Principal at Corentyne Comprehensive Secondary school, as well as acting Principal at the said school. Because of medical reasons she retired and we migrated to the USA in 1999 and still reside here.

Rose Hall high School was founded in 1958 by Mr. Rudra Nath- - a man with a vision and determination. He was an outstanding human being with great humility, love and compassion for others. Whenever we meet we would sing his praise and reflect on his wonderful contributions he had made in our lives and the community as a whole.

I would like to thank all teachers for their dedication and hard work. They were able to fulfill the teachers' motto: 'to mold the nation'. Thank you Mr. Hari for making "an educational journey against all odds possible". I assure you this book will live on from generation to generation---a great contribution and a wonderful legacy.

AZIM AND EVA EOONOUS

Before   After

Life's journey is often dictated by events that may not necessarily be apparent at the time of their occurrences, but they assume great significance and importance with the passage of time. Growing up in Guyana at a time when secondary education was a luxury of the well to do, Rose Hall High School was inaugurated by an individual, Mr. Rudra Nath, who could be easily classified as a Philanthropist by today's standard for all the good work he performed on behalf of the community. He provided affordable access to secondary education for those who craved the opportunity. He was supported by a dedicated staff that was genuinely interested in providing the best educational opportunities for the students whose academic pursuit and success were not constrained by time or ability to pay but one's drive and determination to succeed.

Many students took advantage of this opportunity, and for some, their destiny was imbedded in the longevity that life affords them. Eva and I were among the many who capitalized on this opportunity.

After my graduation, I taught school for a while and was later married to my high school class mate, Eva Bhairo, who also graduated from Rose Hall High, now called Corentyne Comprehensive Institute. She also taught school in Corentyne before we transferred to schools in Enterprise and Enmore to facilitate my attendance at the University of Guyana.

We then moved to Canada for graduate studies. Upon our return to Guyana and following a short stint as an Economic Adviser to the Minister of Economic Development, I assumed the position of Chief Executive Officer of the Guyana Manufacturers' Association. I also served in a similar capacity with the Lyson's Group of Companies until we migrated to the United States. We settled in Connecticut, where I was employed by an aeronautical company while Eva worked at Trinity College in Hartford. Later, we relocated to Florida to take advantage of the tropical climate.

While in Florida, I was employed as a Non-instructional Administrator with the Miami Dade School System until I retired. Eva worked with the Hospital District until she retired early to take care of the grandchildren.

Rose Hall High was a significant determinant in initiating our pursuit for higher education fostering our family relationship and positively impacting our future. We are now retired and we commute between South and Central Florida to spend quality time with our son, his spouse and five children in Ocala and our daughter who is located in Orlando. We are also grateful for this opportunity to express our sincere appreciation to the late Mr. Rudra Nath, the Staff and the entire student body. We are indeed thankful that we had the opportunity to meet Mr. Nath on several occasions in South Florida. Our gratitude is also extended to the Organizer of this project for providing this avenue for a nostalgic review of the good old days and the very many unforgettable memories.

HARDATT ETWAROO

This is a brief experience that I had at Rose Hall High school.

On Sept. 4, 1961 I entered for the first time the classroom at RHS to form 2 at the concrete building at Rose Hall waterside (as it was called, should have been called the foreshore). Raised by parents of meager means my main objective was to ace through school as quickly as possible, hence my focus was direct… Get an education and become a teacher.

From Form111, I was accorded a promotion into Form iv. Hence I skipped Form 111. In Form iv I became acquainted with Chattergoon, a great fellow. He defended me when a student, whom I shall call Bhago, butted a cigarette on my forehead because I refused to smoke. Chattergoon pushed him against the window of the new RHS wing. In the construction of the new school building, we worked to make cinder blocks, wheel barrowed sand etc to build this new wing. Had some unforgettable experience in class. In our Geography class with Mr. Naidoo (our teacher) we had to prove that the world is round. My friend, Boodoo, was asked to explain. He stood up and said 'this man proved that the world is round because he juked three posts and the middle one was higher. This proved the world is round'. Jokingly, Mr. Naidoo asked him what does 'juk' mean? He proudly demonstrated by showing the motions of planting a post.

Further, indelibly engraved is an issue where one of the female students said something to my friend which made him grin without stopping. The then Teacher, Mr. Rawana asked what was so funny? He replied in his best possible English. "She told me…" He was asked repeatedly, what "she told you"? Subsequently, he replied exactly, "s—t hold me"

I don't want to add too much, but to say, I next advanced to grade vi. Studied hard and wrote GCE in June,'64 sitting at Belvedere Comprehensive High School. What a disaster for me. I wrote 7 subjects. Completed my answers quickly, accurately and handed in my booklet. Felt great. Expected excellent results. DISASTROUS results. On 5 subjects my results were DNA (did not appear). I was devastated. My parents, included my Grandparents, were furious, accusing me of wasting their money. I did not do that. I was simply cheated (will clarify later). Prior to our writing exams we were displaced to the grand stand of Port Mourant race tracks. Was very difficult to concentrate, but determination was my driving force. School was subsequently relocated to the factory building of Port Mourant Sugar Factory. Our principal, Mr Nath heard the news of my DNA. Assistant Principal, V. Asregadoo, consoled me by promising to write to the University of London to determine my result. No luck.

I believe you can recall the newspaper head line 'gross misconduct at GCE exams'. I excelled in Math and English Language, the two subjects that were graded. Because of this mishap, I did not return to school but studied on my own privately and re-wrote exam in

January,'65-66. Got excellent grades with a pass in 4 subjects but failed history.

Remained at home year, (65-66). Planted rice, reared sheep and goats. Flooded all possible potential employers with applications. No luck until end of May, 1966, when I went to Georgetown Rice Marketing Board to pick up cheques for our sale of rice, because in those days cheques were crossed and mailed. My Mamoo and myself made our way to G/T and presented ourselves at the counter, where we were issued cheques for my Dad and Grand-dad. On leaving, we ran into no other but Mohamed Raufman. He was working at RMB. Of course the obvious question, " Et., What are you doing"? My reply was, somewhat subdued, as I was embarrassed to say I was a rice farmer, although my credentials were very good. Before leaving, Mohamed ID'd my cheques which made them cashable. We cashed the cheques then proceed to check job prospects at the GPO (General Post Office), Public Service Commission on the status of my application. We met Mr. Skeetes, who surprised me with the news that he was in the process of sending out my appointment letter with a confirmed posting in Georgetown. Before I could say I did not want to work in G/T, my Mamoo, (maternal uncle) replied that he will take it. I had no say hence on June 6, 1966 (6-6-66) I entered the Classified Public Service in Guyana in the Dept. of Agriculture, the lands and mines division.

Subsequently, during my working, I ran into a policeman, the same guy whom I called Bhago. He was new in G/T and I became his friend with a few drink sessions. On one of those sessions, he confessed that he was the one who had 'stolen' my exam booklets and destroyed them. It is possible as my name being Etwaroo, his very similar, he told me he could not have completed his answers, and as such as soon as I tendered my booklets, he followed and on leaving simply took my answer books which were on top of the pile.

It cost me a year and a half, but he got his just due. I feel sorry for him…and forgave him.

I, on the other hand, met a beautiful girl, fell in love, got married and migrated to Montreal, Canada. Still alive and doing well as a widow with two children and three wonderful grandchildren.

GEORGE GOPIE

THE REFLECTIONS OF THE 60's AT RHS.

Before I begin, let me make a disclosure. All persons mentioned are real, and it's not meant to be funny.It reflects what makes many of us who we are today.

My life begins in a small village in Guyana. My village name was No.60 village. My parents were farmers. They were engaged in rice farming, vegetable gardening, and fishing, and especially harvesting of shrimp. Many of the villagers were alike in many of their daily functions.

My parents, like many other parents wanted the best for their children, and particularly wanted them to go to school. Their method of motivating their children was not based on social motivation. There was not too much praise for work at school. Their method of motivating you was to allow you to find out how hard it is to work in the rice fields, and gardening for your livelihood.

I was ten or eleven years old, and I had to work with my parents in the rice field, pulling out weeds called "hiss be zee".

The 60's in High School was a hard time. The focus of parents, teachers, relatives, and students were to be successful at the GCE and Cambridge Examinations.

Trail blazers were Mr. Basil Jagernauth, Mahadeo Rajdhanny, Rai Ramsagar, and Khublall Ramrattan. In those days, no one was identified as your mentor, but I'll let you know that Basil Jagernauth was my mentor, because he was so good in Math, and then he recommended Trantor, Advanced Level Mathematics Text to me.

All of us had our favorite teacher/s. I will highlight my favorite, the late Mr. Gajraj Ramnarine.Gaj was our our Mathematics teacher in fifth form. Slow and deliberate, he would take his time in presenting topics in Geometry, Algebra and Arithmetic. I remember very vividly, the proof of the Pythagoras Theorem. I mean the proof, and not the formula, as many colleges and university students would spout out as a squared plus b squared equal c squared. As a matter of fact, my son who was in his senior year in college doing physics, had some of his friends over at the house and I asked them if they know how to prove the Phythagoras Theorem. Of course out came the formula. Where is Bharrat Latchman when I need him? I can say without being too arrogant that when it comes to Geometry Riders, Gaj. knew that Bharrat and myself will have the proof.

Mr. Ramanrine, drew the right triangle and completed the squares on each side. He then proceeded to divide all the squares into smaller triangles. Each triangle was numbered for identification. He demonstrated which triangles were equal in area, and thus prove the theorem. My son and his friends from VT University were visiting and I asked if they can prove Pythagoras theorem. They look at me in amazement, and just blurted out the formula. It just goes to show the depth of our high school knowledge, and the dedication of our teachers.

I was able to use the same principle when I went to get my Teaching license in New York City, and the interviewer asked me where I learn this.... and so Mr. Gajraj Ramnarine still lives.

Riding bicycles was the major method of getting to and from school. There were brand names like, Humber, Raleigh, Rudge, and many others.

The first psychedelic bikes were being ridden to the swamp at RHS. When Pamela and her late sister Iona rode their bikes to school, it was a gathering to behold because of the colors on their bikes.

You cannot in those days know the influence of your teachers. When Mr, Yassim Sankar started his first history lesson and just the vocabulary he used blew us away. Words like ecclesiastic would peak the interest of many students. Mohanlall Sukhai and Prema Sukra excelled in History.

What about GIV...Mr. Kempadoo the best dressed student. He would iron his pants everyday and when he sat in class his legs were never bent, so he can keep the seam unbroken. Where is Ronald Budwah? I could not believe that anyone could have written essays so perfectly. We used his essays as model answers. Remember model answers.

After the sweat, and the   bingo, Shakepspeare plays of many students, especially Soman Lall, Ramesh Jhagroo, Madho, Ajib, Bansraj, Bill Jute and host of others (parents and students) we were able to complete the indoor toilets at the Swamp. We were elated that now we have indoor toilets, but unfortunately we could not do one crap (literally) in them, because we were heading for Port Mourant Race Course to continue our education.

Chunmattie Gurbatur

In the mid-fifties, there became a great emphasis on education for female students. After a few visits from J.R Latchmansingh, the Headmaster of Albion C.M School, I had no alternative but to adhere to the rules that were set by my father. My two sisters before me were already married at the ages of fifteen and sixteen respectively. My mother's philosophy on a girl's life is, she should learn household chores and be prepared to be a wife, a mother and a homemaker. My father insisted that "Education is a Passport to a successful future". And so, I travelled on a daily basis from Rose Hall Village to Albion Estate and in my two senior years, I was able to achieve The School Leaving Certificate of Education and the Pupil Teachers' Certificate. Gardening, Home Economics and Sewing were also great achievements, but, I was now on top of the world, no more school. I will wear regular dresses and I will be allowed to go to the local cinemas with new friends I had made.

But of course, freedom of thought was short- lived. There came the dedicated teacher, Harold Appadu, who advised my father to send me to RN in Port Mourant. Within two months, the avid campaigner,Harold Appadu, already spoke on behalf of my father, to enroll me at RHS.The following are the first students that graced the attendance register: - Arjoonan Permaul, Ronald Guizar, Kampta Persaud, Ganpat Chunoo, H.Balgobin ,Ivan Fitzcummings Harry,Clifford Manns, Hugh Todd Williams ,Henry Chisolm, Marcia Evans, Pansy Beharry, Ormin Austin, Sirpattie Mangar and Yachumatty Gurbatur .The enthusiasm was great and the quest for secondary education reflected on every expression and physical movements of our being. Most of us were transferred from RN School of Book keeping and Learning.

Yes, we are now all high school students and under the leadership of Rudra Nath and his dedicated team of Udai Panday and Adarsh Hari lecturing began cautiously and some ways aggressively. We, the students bonded and great friendships were created and have lasted for five decades. The teachers: - Adarsh K Hari, Vernon Asregadoo, Raymond Singh, Haman Ben Yassim, and later William Rawana and Julius Nathoo are to be credited with the great successes of the first College of Preceptors and Senior Cambridge Examinations. At the start of RHS it was the very young Adarsh K. Hari who championed the subject of Latin. His dedication was immense and is part of the original team. I do thank Mr. Vernon Asregadoo for my two distinctions in English language which motivated me to attend the University of Toronto and obtain a degree in Mass Communications.

After graduation, most of the female students became school teachers and most important nurses; also the majority became wives, mothers and raised very good families. A few of the male students did become nurses as well as school teachers, also quite a number of them worked as civil servants in the government services. I also became a teacher at St. Francis Xavier Roman Catholic School, and within a few years migrated to Canada. I also became a successful mother of five.

In the very near future, most of the former students migrated to the United Kingdom, North America and various parts of the world. Successes were measured in 1995 when there was a reunion for the students of all three institutions. In this event 228 students reunited with one another. They shared their experiences and their added life achievements. My journey at Rose Hall High School was very successful and accolades to the founder and his original team for guiding us through this journey.

CHANDRA HANOMAN RAMKUMAR

MY MEMORIES OF THE ORIGINAL

ROSE HALL HIGH SCHOOL

Rose Hall High School has and will have a very, very special place in my heart. I think all us who started at this school in 1959 have a very unique bond that no one can understand except us. It has been a special, life-long bond with wonderful memories. We worked very hard but we also had a lot of fun. Here are some memories as I remembered:

I graduated from elementary school in 1958 and was at home for a year because Corentyne High School was not taking in new students due to lack of space at that school. I always wanted to further my education and when Rose Hall High school opened in 1959, I felt it was God sent. I will always be indebted to Mr. Rudra Nath for his dedication to education. He was a very caring man who greatly improved the lives of those who were fortunate to know him and attend this school at that time.

The pioneers of this school were Mr. Rudra Nath, Mr. Adarsh Hari, Mr. Panda, and Mr. Banerjee. I started in Form 1 in 1959 and was promoted to Form 2 within 2 months. I was again moved to Form 4 within a year. Mr. Nath was trying to get a group of us to write the College of Preceptors exam within 2 years, thus the moving forward of some students. We did write that exam within two years (1961) and had resounding success-- over 90% passed the exam! I think this exam was usually written after 3 years of high school but we did it in 2 years. This was when the name of RHS took off and the attendance grew rapidly.

As the enrollment grew, Mr. Nath, Mr. Hari, Mr. Banerjee, Mr. Panday and the newer teachers- Mr. Vernon Asregadoo, Mr. Raymond Singh, Mr.Milton Latcha, Mr. Julius Nathoo etc. started doing fund raising to build a bigger school because space was a problem at the original school. Students and teachers held many concerts and other events to raise funds for this cause. There were many volunteers.

The students came out every Saturday to help with the building of our new school. I think we all took pride in helping--I know I did. The teachers were all there working right along with us. We were truly a special group of people. We took such pride in helping in whatever way we could. I had never worked with cement before but learned quickly!

I do not know what most of us would have done or where we would have ended up, had it not been for Rose Hall High School and the wonderful caring teachers we were all lucky to have. I ended up studying for my GCE Exam on my own while I had a teaching job at Albion Government School from 1962. I studied at nights and taught school during the day. I left Guyana in 1965 for Ireland where I went to College and Radiography School. I returned to Guyana in 1969 and worked as a radiographer at Georgetown and New Amsterdam hospitals until1975 when I got married and came to the USA.

I worked at the Hamilton Hospital here for 24 years. I continued in the Radiography path & got certified in Mammography, CT and Ultrasound. I was promoted to Director of Radiography in 1991. I was on the Radiography Advisory Board at the college nearby. I was also a Clinical Instructor for radiography students. I would not have reached this level in my career had it not been for the great foundation I received from Mr. Nath and the wonderful teachers of Rose Hall High School. I am now retired and still live in Iowa.

Special thanks and appreciation to the late Mr. Rudra Nath! Mr. Hari - you were the most loyal teacher who stayed from the beginning to the end, helping and tutoring us. You made Anatomy so easy for me when I entered the medical field because many of the names of words in Anatomy and Physiology are derived from Latin words. All of us who attended RHS those first few years have been extremely successful in our careers and we could not have done this without our wonderful teachers.

Mr. Hari, here you are again with us wanting to put our memories together. It is not an easy task to get in touch with everyone. I am very thankful and grateful to you for doing this. We can all have our memories in one book. I am looking forward to this book which I will treasure. Thank you, thank you and God bless you for all you have done for all of us!

ADARSH KUMAR HARI'S

CONTRIBUTION

Before   After

I, Adarsh Kumar Hari, was born at Uitvlugt, West Coast Demerara. My early years were extremely challenging. My experiences gave me a better concept of life and enriched me with a greater understanding of it.

I attended the G. R Dwarka's school for underprivileged children and here I was awarded the Walter Guyadeen's scholarship to attend Guyana's Oriental College (a High School) in Georgetown for four years. I did not realize at first that getting an education required so much sacrifice. I was determined to give it my all. During these four years, I had to be up at 5 in the morning and traveled 2 miles from home to the train station and then traveled 15 miles by train, plus an extra half hour by ferry, and then an additional 2 miles to school. This was my routine for four years. At school, I gave it all I could, never lightening up. The boat in which I was traveling through these four years I call, study, and I rode it hard with never a relaxed moment.

Following graduation, Rudra asked me to join him and another teacher, Odai Panday, to start a high school in Corentyne Berbice. In September, 1958 our school became officially opened to the public. I was only 18, with no formal teaching experience, but I decided to give it my best shot. I believed in my heart that this was my grand opportunity to serve. I trusted the Lord to guide me.

For 10 years, I taught in the halls of learning, and here I saw the hunger, thirst, and passion for education. These 10 years were years of unforgettable memories. I saw our students facing tremendous odds - poor economic condition, inadequate educational standards, crowded and poorly equipped classrooms, and unfavorable environments and much more. Yet, despite these odds, our students with their unswerving determination, with a focused, yet, undaunted spirit and ambition were able to face these insurmountable challenges and win the crowns of success -achievements worthy of their struggles.

In April 1970, after a journey of 10 years at RHS, PMCI and CCHS, I decided to leave a successful career and pursue a higher education abroad in the USA. Life here was extremely difficult for me. With no money and a large debt, I had to find a job. I worked 60 hours a week while attending the University and taking 18 hours per semester. With hard work my debts were paid off. I also graduated with my Bachelor's and Master's degrees -the latter in Educational Psychology and Counseling. During this time, at the University, I was the president of the foreign students' Club for two years.

Immediately upon graduation, I became a counselor in St.

Paul, Minnesota for the Urban League. After two years at St. Paul, Minnesota, I moved to Houston, Texas with my family. I took up a teaching assignment in Houston and taught for 15 years until my retirement. I am now enjoying the sunset years of my life.

In reflecting on my life, I have made wonderful inroads of successes on the travel log of time and have garnered wonderful memories in the many ventures of my life. However, the journey at RHS, PMCI and CCHS has had a tremendous impact on me. It has been a significant part of my life -- a very remarkable and rewarding experience. I have seen how the lives of both students and teachers have changed through the years. Today, they are playing important and significant roles in today's society. Yes, they have offered their unique contributions while making a tremendous impact on the family and the community.

In capturing the special moments of my life, I feel so very blessed to have been a part of so many lives who have never been the same since they themselves walked through the halls of learning at these schools and, who now have become pillars of success in today's societies.

GANESH HARILAL

In Guyana, there is a saying that in order to have a strong and healthy plant, you have to create an environment in which the plant can strive and grow to become tall, mature and well rounded. My view of education is the same. A school has to have an environment that is conducive to learning, growing and developing a culture that not only motivate students, but leave them with lifelong experiences. Although resources were limited, the environment at Port Mourant Comprehensive School created that special something that made me look back as a student with a sense of excitement, nostalgia and belonging.

I began attending Comprehensive High School in the early sixties. We were located at the Port Mourant Race Course. At first glance, it seems awful attending high school at a Race Course and having classes in the pavilions. But no, when I look back at my experiences, these were the best of times in my educational development. The way I reflect upon this period is that the Race Course offered us a certain environmental freedom. We were in the open, in the middle of nature, looking out as far as the eye can see. We were not curtailed, as in the traditional classroom, looking at four walls. Our classroom, form two, was located in the small pavilion to the extreme north. When the rain poured, we huddled in the center of the class because the northern side and top seats became soaked with water. This, however, was not a problem: we loved the rain because it gave us the opportunity to move closer to the girls in the front benches! I can still, vividly, see my classmates all giggling with excitement at the assembling of rainclouds. I also recall, very fondly, the horses and the riders practicing in the morning, the versatile singing of English songs during breaks by one of a senior student from Tarlogie. Students would gather around him, by the rails, on the actual Race Course to listen to him. His voice would carry all the way to the stands creating a sort of serenity and forcing one to look up to trace the source of the song.

In the ideal world of education as we know it today, the open environment, the horses, the rain, the structure of the classrooms, would be considered distractions to learning. In my experience at the Race Course, I would argue the opposite: that the Race Course molded us into a more disciplined group of students. Emile Durkheim, a noted sociologist hypothesized that a positive environment makes us into a more "socially integrative" group. Educators have postulated that a society that is socially integrated is more successful in producing high achievers. Comprehensive was such a school!

After about two semesters, we moved from the Race Course to the current location of Comprehensive. While not an open environment compared to the Race Course, it was, nevertheless, educationally friendly. There were two buildings at the beginning: the main building with the classrooms and the office with the asbestos sheets covering the roof. A third building was built very quickly and our form three was moved into it. Teacher Surujpaul Jatischand (Cats) and later Mr. James Permaul were my class masters.

The years at Comprehensive, before we wrote GCE, were full of fun. I used to look forward to participating in sports like volley ball and high jumping. Our coach Chando, a teacher, was an excellent volley ball player, moving swiftly, like a shadow, across the court to defend a ball spiked by the other side. At recreation, we would go under a tree where the old Port Mourant factory was, to eat lunch and socialize. Over here, in North America, this is equivalent to taking a walk in the woods, a luxury many cannot afford.

Sociologists and Political Scientists have delineated four factors that are most influential in our life, referred to as the socialization process. These factors are family, school, education, media and peer group. My education at Comprehensive, upon reflection, has been the single most important factor that has prepared me for later accomplishments. The didactic approach to education as opposed to the now more "cooperative or participatory" style prepared students very well. It created excitement and motivation. I recall the debates, we as students, use to have, in regards to English, Literature, History and Politics.

Teachers are most crucial in influencing students and high school is a representation of the formative years, in terms of the development of one's views. This is why many look back at their high school days with deep emotions and sentimentality. This is how I feel about Comprehensive.

The mark of a very good school is the attachment and excitement it leaves with its student. For me, Comprehensive has left a permanent nostalgic vision of the teachers, the students, the principal, the office workers and the environment. It was a great experience and I am grateful to have been part of this institution.

Ganesh Harilal* Professor, Political Science Vanier College, Montreal

DAVENDRA (BRAZO) HARIPERSAUD

Rose Hall high school was founded in 1958 by Mr. Rudra Nath, an educator of outstanding class. The establishment of Rose Hall High School was to fulfill the dire need for many primary school leavers who could not find a place in the only high school, Corentyne High School in the area.

Imbued with a pioneering spirit towards education, Mr. Nath persuaded a businessman to rent the Rock Diamond Hotel building to start the school. Initially, the school had about 25 students and within a year, the student population grew with amazing rapidity.

The Rock Diamond Hotel building could not accommodate the students comfortably so efforts were made to have a more spacious building. Mr. Rudra Nath was fortunate to secure a tract of land at the Rose Hall Reef, five blocks away from the main public road. On this plot of land, parents, community, well-wishers, students and teachers, volunteered to build a new high school, an L-shaped concrete building. Funds from organized school events, teachers monthly (a $10.00 cash donation), parents' contributions as well as donations from civic minded individuals and supporters went towards the building construction.

As the building was in its final phase of completion and the golden moment was imminent for its official opening, trouble erupted between Rudra, the Principal and the Board of Governors. In the interim, between the initial phase of construction and its final phase of the completion of the building, the Board of Governors was conspicuously inactive. This however, did not significantly detract the teachers from teaching and the students from learning.

Teachers taught with great fervor and students reciprocated by performing satisfactorily at both the Senior Cambridge and the London University GCE 'O' level exams. Students' successes and achievements at these examinations were viewed by the Board without merits and tensions between the principal and this governing body reached boiling point in 1963.

The Board wanted full control of the running and administration of the school and Mr. Nath would not comply. This led the Board of Governors to throw tantrums and they decided to settle this in court. The Board of Governors was able to secure an injunction against the principal from entering the school. The teachers got to know about this and they acted.

Teachers sought a meeting with the Board of Governors. At this meeting the teachers requested solid proofs to support their actions against the principal. None was given. The Board members were completely out of their minds and could not read into the teachers and students minds who publicly demonstrated and held meetings. At one such meeting the 'death of the Board of Governors' was announced and the teachers, students and Principal vacated the

Rose Hall High School building.

Students, teachers, principal, and ancillary staff moved to the Port Mourant Race Course Pavillions.Though the students were affected, they showed determination and performed very well at their GCE 'O' level examination, taken in June,1963. Many students reached great heights becoming lawyers, teachers, university graduates, politicians, nurses etc. Others with similar education background went into the trades, business and agriculture.

In 1964, a merger with Comprehensive Institute, a newly established learning unit, about half a mile from the Port Mourant Race Course Pavilions, was successfully concluded between Mr Rudra Nath and the Founders of the Comprehensive Institute, a new name was given- Comprehensive High School with Rudra as Principal.

Comprehensive High School did very well at the examinations (College of Preceptors and the GCE 'O' level examinations) as well as in the sports. It could boast of having molded some of the finest academic minds in the agrarian community and East-West Berbice areas. It also nurtured some outstanding sportsmen of international fame and stature.

While all of these ongoing activities and events were taking place, the Board of Governors at Rose Hall High School, having crossed a civilized boundary, was left with a vacant building.

Mr. Rudra Nath was a person of great humility, love, compassion and honesty. He served with distinction. The teachers and students love and admire him. When teachers and students meet his name would come up for discussions and these discussions would reflect on his wonderful contributions he made for the upliftment of a community crying out for help.

Mr. Rudra Nath resigned in March 1966 and was succeeded by Mr. Walter Ramdehol (BSc. Economics, London). He went on to establish another school in the area since Comprehensive High School could not accommodate the vast number of school leavers who were coming from primary schools and who were thirsty for a secondary education.

TO KILL A DREAM

BY JODHAN J HEERAMAN

"Fees were not important ..... what was important is that the children of the poor should have an [opportunity] at   education . . . . at least in Berbice." (Moses Nagamootoo).

I am honored to have been afforded an exposure to culture and Asian Language that were never offered at CHS – these blended my character to who am I this day? Above all else, we had a 'universal prayer' that distinguishes no ethnicity yet embraces all creeds; this was an idea before our time. These are memories that refuse to fade away but flourish with every renewed acquaintance that places one in a moment in time that freezes, and an embrace that reinforces that lingered dream.

Notwithstanding the fluctuations of student life at RHS (where the name of the institution changed so many times, classes under the mango tree, music on the tin roof with 'raindrops falling on [our] head[s]', with birds chirping and students eloping to start something fresh, and bees competing for the most attractive buttercup as teachers getting married to their students), is as memorable as the day my Ma gave birth to her son.

A Dream Is Born

Coming from a struggling Farmer's home in pastoral Corentyne on the Atlantic coast of Northern South America, I was destined, not unlike the many poor children, for an agrarian life on the sugar plantation of Port Mourant. But as WILL shall determine, that destiny was altered when the "School Leaving" exams results for Tain Govt. School was published in the Guyana Graphics listing Janak Jodhan, the only pass for that year. My class Master and role model, Mr. Fredrick Ross had earlier visited and begged my parents, "You must send this boy to High School; he must go to Chandisingh School." My Papa mellowed and wished not to challenge Mr. Ross. Ma pinched the pennies, sold a couple of hogs and then borrowed what was short for the entrance and first term fees (payable in advance). I felt previledged registering at Corentyne High School (CHS) for that was what the school represented – the priveliged class!

With white short sleeved shirt, navy blue striped tie and above-knee trousers, with a pair of second-hand brown loafers (souls worn), I started high school at Chandisingh at age 15, not the usual age (this, another untold story). The loafers were tight for my scattered, expanded toes (not used to foot ware). First midterm one Saturday morning, after feeding the hogs and letting the sheep out to the pasture, I returned home to find this intimidating, neatly dressed, but modest little man chatting with my folks at the entrance of the Grass House – our magnificent edifice.

AN EDUCATION COMPROMISED

"Dis ah Mr. Nath; e from da new skool ah Rose Hall." Ma introduced me to this small man and as he offered his hand and I extended mine, I experienced a first firm and memorable handshake. Persuasive and to the point, Mr. Nath spared no philosophy to convince my parents that I must switch to Rose Hall High (RHS) – "… much lower fees..", said he. The campaigner seemed rushed; I imagined the entourage had many more homes targeted for new students. I was stuck between a rock and not so easy spot; what do I say to my mentor, Mr Ross, when he sees me in a different colored uniform! At CHS I was settled and comfortable with my teachers and fellow students, and my girlfriend in the neighboring class? And then, another visit from Rudra the following week! My family's financial profile must have been transparent and the much lower school fees – that nailed the Chandisingh coffin for me – I closed that brief paragraph of my schooling. I interrupted my studies in mid-term, switched to RHS, and no one said that was ill-advised; no one recommended completing the semester at CHS before moving on to RHS.

ROMANCING AN EDUCATION

After spending about six weeks in Form II, on the recommendation of Adarsh K. Hari, literature master, Mr. Nath placed me in a higher class – accelerated promotion – I was told. "You are too old and too smart to be in Form II." After completing Form III at the top of the class, and one semester in the fourth form, I was again accelerated in preparation for GCE (London's General Certificate of Education).

The student population had outgrown the school's capacity on several fronts. The school needed more classrooms, more chalk boards, furniture and washrooms. A very diplomatic and modest demand of the students' involvement in "self-help" (to maintain the still low school fees) was sounded. Most senior students and some faculty members responded enthusiastically to these calls for sacrifices. I became a part-time construction worker after classes at 15:00hrs, and with changing clothes now being stuffed daily into my school bag, studies were compromised often without parents' knowledge. (Pity, now today's HS seniors fetch extra towels and pillows.) And on Fridays, we would spend all night turning spades and doing masonry, as we involuntarily build muscles, to beat the timetable for the completion of the new facilities – 'flush toilets'. However, pit latrines were never threatened, they would continue to serve the needs for the next generation of students. What this modernization means for many was less use of 'exercise leaf!'

I remember one Top Side student (Upper Corentyne), after using the 'modern facilities', retired to the outhouse to soap his finger. As I enquired about his embarrassment, he responded: "Bhai, every time me tear one sheet and wipe, me finger bore right through the thin paper and get shit!" He used single perforated tissue sheet to wipe and thought he was not supposed to 'waste the toilet paper'. This must have been misconstrued from the many lectures our Principal would deliver in a week on economics, culture, mannerism, and hygiene. What a hilarious embarrassment!

RUDRA, THE EDUCATOR

As a principal and educator Rudra Nath's style and effectiveness were unchallengeable for his era. However, as an administrator and manager, he was confrontational when misunderstood, possessed of stubborn tenacity; perhaps a man before his time. Many who worked with Rudra failed to understand that he never considered himself a businessman; he was never in the 'business' of education, his was the Orwellian approach, the philosophy of affordable education for all social classes accompanied by self-indulgence and personal sacrifices. The rumor mills circulated stories of strife amongst the alleged educators whom the student body were unaware of and never met. The Board of Governors presented non-negotiable conditions for the Principal to be subjected to and this aggravated the already sour relationship with the servant and his staff. As the strife with the governing body became public knowledge and the principal preoccupied, education was placed at risk. These visible interruptions continued with stinging effects on student studies and so they were offered a choice to remain at RHS or relocate to some uncertain location with the Principal and most of the staff. And thus began a nomadic life and dispersed education process that would not fail to leave permanent scars on many students' dreams.

Many years later I would indulge A.S Neil's radical approach to education - "Summer Hill" (where Britain's high schools dropouts are offered a second chance) and RHS surfaced back into my world, causing huge goose bumps. "Summer Hill" provoked bitter-sweet memories from my early high school years at RHS and presented Rudra Nath in a different perspective. In the colonial Commonwealth, Rudra was to education what Cromwell was to the birth of democracy in England. I must say, that there will be very few who would have crossed Rudra's path and not be profoundly influenced. The character had such a persona!

Despite the honorable intent, the Herculian efforts, the communities support, and the unselfish staff and teachers, the many challenges facing the school and its principal seemed ungracious. However, many would achieve excellence and successes. In the 1989 'Teacher of the Year Award' at the White House, President George Bush honored a teacher, from American Virgin Island. Mohanlall Birbahadur was the teacher and a product of Rose Hall High School.

BASIL JAGARNATH.

MOMENTS TO REMEMBER AT RHS

Sweet, sweet are the memories. However, high school life is not always fun. Students are sent to school to study. Problems, like no or late assignments, difficult examinations, brain crashing, low and failing grades, being disciplined and many more cannot be avoided.

At St. Joseph's Primary School, I was successful at the Pupil Teachers' Examinations, but was unable to find a job. Schools were, then, controlled by the Church. I remained at home for two years, assisting my mother in the fields. High School education seemed to be unattainable.

However, one early morning, my neighbor, Mr. Rahaman, shouted for me. "Do me a favor. Take this letter to Mr. Nath, the Principal of Rose Hall High School and wait for a response." I wasunaware of the content of the letter. I immediately left for Mr. Nath's home. He was in the shower. I waited patiently. He took the letter, read it and asked," do you want to attend High School?" The response was obvious. I was happy. This happiness vanished in seconds. Fees had to be paid. Books had to be bought. My mother was the lone wage earner of a family of six.

I hurried home. Dressed with whatever was available and with a few note books given to me by my Primary School's Head Master, I left for Rose Hall High School. I was placed in the 1st Form. Mr.Ben Yassim was the Form Master. It was the end of the year, so I had to take the final examinations.

On returning to school for the new school year, I was promoted to the 3rd Form. Here, I was in the company of a wonderful bunch of students. Both boys and girls were so well knitted, so socially integrated, that we help each other in times of difficulties. Wasn't this, or isn't this, one of the objectives of education? Kamal Ramsagar Rai and Rohini Jagpot were among the 'high fliers.' Bill Jhoot, Harold Sukhai, Rudolph Mendonca, Sheik Ishmael and Joshua Ramsammy, were my 'buddies.' This relationship continued for a long time. All six of us escaped from school on one Friday afternoon, only to return at 2pm. when school would be dismissed at 2:30 pm. We were disciplined. All of us were lined up in front of the class. Parents were contacted.

At this period of time, also, the teachers and students were involved in fund raising activities to assist in the construction of a new building at the Rose Hall Swamp Section. Here, I was taught to make concrete hollow blocks. We attended school in the day, make tiles from 6pm to 8pm and on Saturday and Sunday, some students and teachers travelled to different parts of the country to sell raffle tickets and to take part in concerts. Yes, we were on our way to be fully molded, to shoulder responsibilities. Weren't we receiving an all-round education?

I continued to move on. I was promoted from the 3rd Form to the 5th Form. Here, I was in the company of a new set of friendly and well-motivated students - Arjunen Permaul, Kamta Persaud, Parasar, Chunoo, Manns, Khuba, Harry, Mohanlall Birbahadur, Vera De Groot

Chumattee, Chandra Ramkumar and Kamal Ramsagar Rai. Most, if not all, were successful at the College of Preceptors Examinations. After leaving Primary School, these students could not gain a place in High School, perhaps, because of financial restraints or a shortage of places in High Schools. Most remained at home, working in the fields or doing odd jobs. Didn't Mr. Nath, satisfy one of the very important needs of the society by starting a High School in the area? We were a good group. No student was regarded as a social outcast. One day, a student, had a page with girls in swimsuits. He wrote something on the page, passed it around to the girls. This landed in the hands of Mr. Nath, The Principal. All the boys were taken outside, lined up and questioned. No one squealed.

Here, I took part in my first debate. Vera De Groot, Arjunen and I made up the team for the 5th Form, going against the 4th Form, my very good friends. The debate was exciting. We won. My good friends in Form 4 claimed that I was responsible for their loss.

At the end of the year, we wrote the Senior Cambridge Examinations. The School did very well. I was invited by Mr. Nath to join his Staff of Teachers. (My first month's salary was used to pay my long over-due school fees.) This was the beginning of a long career in the teaching profession, thirty-four years in Guyana and sixteen years in New York City. I graduated with a B.A., a Post Graduate Diploma in Education at the University of Guyana and an M.A. at the Brooklyn College in New York.

Finally, I wish to express my heart-felt thanks to all my teachers, especially, Mr. Haman Ben Yassim, Mr. Vernon Asregadoo, Mr. Yassin Sankar, Mr. Julius Nathoo, Miss. Prema, Mr. GaJ. Ramnarine, Mr. Milton Latcha, Mr. Raymond Singh and Miss. Norma Bhajan.

A special thanks to Mr. Rudra Nath for affording me the much needed opportunity of pursuing a Secondary Education. He guided and nurtured so many. He has left his footprints on the sands of time. He was selfless and remarkable. He is unforgettable. What would have been our future without Mr. Rudra Nath?

Whoever will read this, to you, I say, follow your dreams. Plan and work vigorously towards your goals. Distractions and obstacles will be many. Persevere and you shall overcome.

RAMESH JAGROO

I started Rose Hall High School at the converted Rock Diamond Hotel may be, in 1959 with Mr. Nath as the principal. During that time, we assisted in the building of our new high school of the same name. Somanlall, Nandlall, myself and several others (both boys and girls) worked very hard in the construction of this school, making concrete blocks, mixing cement and sand and also keeping watch at night to prevent thieves from stealing supplies.

Sometimes after the building was partially completed we moved from the original Rose Hall High School to our new Rose Hall High School. Sometimes later there were some problems between the Principal and the Board of Governors. Consequently, we were forced to move to another location which was the Port Mourant Race Course.The 'Grand Stands 'were converted into classrooms.

I completed high school sometimes in 1963, wrote my GCE exam then left and joined the Guyana police force around March 1964. Six months later, after graduating from the police training school I was assigned to the Brickdam Police Station in Georgetown where I worked for about 2 1/2 years. I then got married on September 4,1966 to a girl from Port Mourant who also attended Rose Hall High School.

I then took a transfer and was assigned to the New Amsterdam Police Station, where I did various types of jobs. The last one was working in the control room. I then resigned in 1969 after which I moved to New York on August 11, 1969. In New York I worked various jobs also. My last job was working with the New York City Transit Authority, where I worked for 25 years with twenty of these years as a supervisor.

I then got sick around March of 2005 and after undergoing several major surgeries I retired in March,2006. By the grace of God, I am doing O.K.I have been still going to the gym and doing lots of prayers. We have two children, one boy, aged 42, and one girl, aged 44, with four grandchildren-- three boys and one girl-- ages: 12,10,9 and 6. In high school, we were five friends who liked five girls, who were also friends. The five guys were married to their five high school sweethearts and they are still married.

JAGAT JAMES

My name is Jagat James. I was born in Port Mourant, Corentyne Berbice, Guyana. I am the eldest son of 12 children born to Duxin, mother) and Ruben James, Father (deceased). My parents call me Charles which became my popular name among friends and family. I now live in Winnipeg, Canada. The rest of my family live in different areas of Canada and the USA. My Mom lives in Toronto, Canada. I have two sisters in Toronto, Canada and three sisters in California. There is also one who lives in Florida, USA. I have a brother also who lives in Mississauga, Canada. Then, there is a brother in Oregon, one in Kentucky, one in New Jersey and one in Jamaica.

We are very blessed to be a large family. There is so much sharing, so much of love so much interaction and so much of struggles. It seems we are always learning from each other and it gives us a great opportunity to strive upwards. We, in our family, have all gone through the rigors of property and extreme struggles but we stick together. Today, we're very integrated and all of us are educated. We have Bachelors degrees, Masters degrees and Doctoral degrees but our deep motivational value is to be there for each other--- what ever the cost. We all believe in education and it was this educational compass that has helped us to travel through the corridors of success and we feel very blessed and thankful that we had the opportunity of getting a good education.

My early years were spent attending Port Mourant Roman Catholic School until the fifth grade then I attended the Port Mourant Anglican school where I completed my primary school education. During my early years I saw the frustration of my father as a cane cutter. My mom would get up at 4 AM in the morning to cook his meals then get it ready for the 5 a.m Estate Truck which took him and others to the cane fields. Dad was most unhappy, miserable, frustrated and depressed. Fortunately, for us mother helped by doing her own business--buying and selling provisions. This helped us survived.

I was determined to free myself and my family from this grave situation and in my heart I believe education was the passport and so when Rose Hall High School came and although it was financially tough for us my parents made the ultimate sacrifice and set the groundwork for their children's education. I was the first to set out to gain a high school education. I started out in 1960 and it was a rough road for me. Studies at school and chores at home was a challenge but I had to create a path to be successful not just for me but because my family depended on my loyalty, dedication and devotion. Not too long after my sister, Leila then my two brothers, Buddy and Anand joined me in this quest.

Our school was growing rapidly and we needed more space. The Principal, Mr. Rudra Nath had a grandiose dream of building a new high school at Rose Hall Village in an area called the 'swamp'. He was going to do it by way of self-help and with the cooperation of the people in the Corentyne area plus the help of students and teachers of the Rose Hall High School. He was an honest man with an open plan and he mesmerized the people on how he would go about doing it. He planned on collecting money from well wishers and doing concerts across the Corentyne area.

I liked his idea and so did hundreds of students, teachers and parents. We formed a social committee of teachers and students where we wrote our own plays which we acted on stage. We also put on concerts with singing and dancing and comedy skits. We were also involved in the actual construction of the school- helping, and loading trucks with sand to fill the low lying areas on which this school was to be built and in mixing cement to make bricks. It was back- breaking work but the unity and strength of the students and teachers and the community were so overwhelming that it seemed like fun rather than work. In no time we had a brand-new L-shaped high school built. It was named Rose Hall High School. I learned a lot from the principai, Mr. Rudra Nath and the teachers about cooperation and the principle of work ethics and self-help.

In 1964 I wrote the GCE 'O' level exam. I was successful and exceedingly happy. I immediately found a job as a reporter with the Mirror Newspaper. I was very fortunate and had the greatest pleasure to have met Dr. Cheddi Jagan whose principles of good doctrine influenced me greatly.

In 1968 I was married to my wife, Bibi and we are blessed with two sons, graduates of the University of Manitoba. I feel so blessed also to have had the rare privilege of sponsoring my mother and my father (deceased), and my four siblings to Canada. Here in Canada I founded the Guyanese Association of Manitoba in January 1978 of which I was the president. This Association was recognized and financed by the government of Canada.

In the course of my journey I wore many hats. I worked for Esso oil company from 1966-1969. I joined the SSJ Lewis in 1969 which traveled extensively in the ports on the Atlantic and Pacific coasts of the West Indies. I also worked at the Motor Coach Industries builders of inner city buses for New Jersey and New York and Greyhound. I retired in 2006 after 33 years of service.

After retirement I am able to explore some of my other desires: traveling, fishing, gardening, reading and writing poetry. Some of my poems include: 'Guyana my home and native land, 'Ode to Port Mourant,'and 'Attribute to womanhood.' I recently wrote a book entitled,' Goodbye, to Port Mourant, Guyana.'

Looking back at the achievements experienced so far in my life I have to say my successes are due solely to my beloved mother and father whose love, guidance and blessings have helped me through all my struggles. It was they who guided my footsteps to Rose Hall High School where I received my education passport that allowed me to travel in all of my life's corridors. I thank them with my whole heart, and a special thanks to Mr. Rudra Nath and his wonderful and dedicated teachers for all their roles they played and finally, to my great Lord for all His guidance and direction in my daily life. I am forever grateful.

Ralph Joseph

By Basant Raj

In the annals of posterity, there never will be a more exalted tale of the sterling contributions Rose Hall High School and Corentyne Comprehensive School have made to the intellectual and social development of yearning students whose dreams and aspirations were meticulously molded under the staunch tutelage of distinguished educators such as Rudra Nath, Walter Ramdehol and Rowtie Kesrielall.

These Stalwarts prophetically exploited the tides of the turbulent times and brought to realization the fruits of success to vast numbers of struggling students. In a time of poverty and despair, they gave hope and sanctity and today their wards are proud ambassadors throughout the world; a fitting accolade of the selfless dedications and dauntless courage of those visionaries and those hallowed institutions.

But under the microcosm of it all, amidst the turmoil of punitive administrations were also many unsung heroes, dedicated individuals from humble beginnings who played pivotal roles in the formative years and exited the instructional arena without any fanfare and fancy exultations. Many revered their duties as educators only and faded into obscurity but their rich legacies will forever live in the malleable minds of those students who were very fortunate to be inspired by such illustrious individuals... one of whom I am indeed proud to bring to focus. Ralph Joseph was born under the zodiac sign of Sagittarius on December 21, 1944 in Whim Village on the Corentyne and had his primary education at Auchlyne Church of Scotland School. As a boy growing up, he had dreams of playing cricket for the dominant Whim Cricket Club but was shrewdly discouraged by his father who was a prominent member of the club then. So with his youthful dream shattered, Joe embarked on devoting his energies to acquiring the skills and prowess of his second choice game, volleyball.

Ironically, Joe initially attended Corentyne High School where he was a Prefect. In 1962 through the kind intervention of Edwin Persram he moved to Rose Hall High School where he became a prominent member of the volleyball team with Hilton Permaul.

In 1963 Joe joined the Police Force where he spent eighteen months until his services were dispensed with; then he started Comprehensive High School in August 1964 on a very ominous note. The times were turbulent as the country was involved in one of its longest industrial strikes in recognition of GAWU and on his first day of school, there was the historic bombing at Tain Koker road in retaliation to scabs taking the jobs of the field workers.

Joe was nineteen years and eight months at that time but that day created and indelible image in his mind as school was cancelled and in the company of Moses Nagamootoo, Hilton Permal and their friends, Joe went drinking. Later, many members of the school staff joined in the revelry which came to a split-bill denouement and Joe became fascinated with the informal teacher/student relationships which were in complete contrast to that which he experienced at

Corentyne High School.

Joe's academic achievements at Comprehensive High School were modest but when Mr. Rudra Nath asked him and a few of his colleagues, including Soman Lall, Moses Nagamootoo, Hilton Permal and Prema Sukra, to join the staff as Student -Teachers he gladly accepted the offer. He was raw but full of enthusiasm and endeavored to make maximum use of that window of opportunity offered to him, and such was his dedication that he focused his attention entirely on achieving success. Joe learned, and learned quickly the basic teaching skills that would become a hallmark of his distinguished teaching career.

Consequently, when the new Principal Mr. Walter Ramdehol took over the school, Joe was the only Student-Teacher who was retained which was a fitting reward for his diligence. From the time Chandradat Narine left Comprehensive to March 1971, Joe was Games Master and he was very instrumental in developing the table tennis skills of Claudwyn Apana, Jainarine Kissoon, Jaglall and Madray. The school also saw its glorious days in cricket, volleyball and table tennis, easily demolishing all rivals within the region. One of the hallmarks of this achievement was that Joe had an inherent ability to spot unique talents very early and was able to nurture those exceptional qualities to excel in any field of endeavor. His dynamism and selfless contribution to the development of sports in the school was a monumental success. In the classroom, Joe taught Geography (and Literature in the second forms) alongside Birbahadur, Naidoo and Chandradat Narine and his competitive nature bore him tremendous recognition. His teaching techniques at that time were unorthodox but they were very effective in a situation where only good results mattered.

Later, as the exodus of Teachers affected staffmg, Joe took up the challenge and began teaching Geography in the senior forms where he attained a fantastic pass rate of 78% which established its reputation with the best before him. His success was inspirational and a legend was born. In March 1971 when the students revolted against the arbitrary imposition of additional games fees by the Comprehensive School Board, in a way they were showing their confidence and appreciation in Joe who was on the firing line. Though the defection was spontaneous, the students' sympathy for him was paramount. His charisma and affability were dominant factors that effected the historic move from Comprehensive back to Rose Hall High School to complete what someone once called " the elongated cycle", simply because the journey would not end there but return to Comprehensive a few years later when the Government nationalized the Schools.

When we reflect on Joe and his meritorious journey from student to teacher to administrator, his strail crosses many boundaries; but his most memorable moments will always be those spent in the classrooms with the students whom he always cares for... and his only regret will be that he cannot relieve that experience ever again.

Today the old Comprehensive School buildings have all been demolished and replaced by modern structures but every student will fondly remember with nostalgia their own Joseph as he was in their mind's eyes, a toothless lion with very strong moral, religious and ethical values who strode those hallowed halls in retrospect of time.

ALVIN KALLCHARAN- COMPRI'S MOST FAMOUS STUDENT

BY RAY SUNDAR

Mike Selvey opined, "Kalli was a touch player who derives his power from his tremendous sense of timing. It helps that he has all the strokes at his disposal and is acknowledged as one of the best players of spin."

The man affectionately known as "Kalli", made his grand entrance into this world on March 21, 1949 to proud parents, Mr. & Mrs.Isaac Kallicharran. As a young lad, he excelled in cricket, and was a fixture, initially at St. Joseph's Anglican Primary School and then Corentyne Comprehensive High School (COMPRI) cricket teams. Many eyes popped and mouths were left ajar, marveling at the strength (technique) of this compact and diminutive left handed fellow who threw the ball farther than any competitor.

At Port Mourant Community Centre Boys Club, he joined forces with several other promising young cricketers- Mohandas Madramootoo, Anand Sookram, Beasmonie, Rishi Jodhan (God rest his soul), Ranji Etwaroo, "Chic" Baldeo (God rest his soul), Stanley Kallicharran (God rest his soul) to form a veritable who is who in school boys cricket in Berbice. After representing Guyana at the highest level of school cricket, at the age of 16 1/2 he became the youngest Guyanese to play in the Shell Shield Tournament.

As it is not my intention to regurgitate his career, I shall touch briefly on some aspects of a splendid career, including his humility and humanitarianism.

He became one of a select few to score a test century on debut. He did the unthinkable in the first innings of his 2nd test, scoring 101 against New Zealand. Consecutive centuries in his first two test innings! Off and running, you say?

During his career he developed a well deserved reputation as one of the best batsmen of spin. Time and again against India, home of the spin gurus, he capably demonstrated this. On December 3 & 5, 1978 in Mumbai against the likes of Bedi, Chandrasekhar and Venkataraghavan, he scored a magnificent 187 (his highest test score), disdainfully dispatching 25x4s to all parts of the boundary.

Though a superb batsman of spin, he showed his impartiality and class by authoring his most ferocious assault against Australia's speed merchant, the glowering and hostile Dennis Lillee. "Standing all of 5 feet 5 inches, hatless and shirt unbuttoned halfway down", this riveting confrontation netted 35 runs for Kallicharran off 10 deliveries in the 1975 World Cup. He extinguished Lillee's fire- hooking, cutting and driving the ball with reckless abandon, clobbering 1x6 and 7x4s, leading the West Indies to victory. One could say Kalli had kangaroo for lunch.

Any tribute to Kalli would be woefully inadequate and totally incomplete without referencing and documenting his humility, his humanitarianism and the respect he engendered.

In 1993 the Sunder family started the annual Harry Sunder

Cricket Match in New York in memory of the family's patriarch. We felt a famous face was an absolute necessity to give the match some much needed star power and a boost which would withstand the test of time. Casting aside some initial skepticism and trepidation I contacted Alvin in England. After articulating my vision, he graciously consented to come to America to lend his name and prestige to the match. When asked about his appearance fee, he responded in a down to earth fashion, "I can't charge you a fee to play in your dad's memorial match. He was a good man. Just provide round trip airline tickets." He came, he played and he conquered. Thousands showed up to see this proud son of the soil of Port Mourant in action. He shook hands, signed memorabilia, exchanged pleasantries, granted interviews to the press folks present etc. Saying the match took off is an understatement of epic proportions. It is now in its 20th year and a must see on NYC's summer calendar.

On another trip to New York, we had lunch at Santoor's restaurant. Grown men from India mobbed him, jumping for joy when he graciously agreed to sign autographs and granting photo ops. Same happened in Florida and Toronto. In Mumbai some acquaintances with ties to Bollywood told me, "Mr. Kalli is here to play in a Masters Cricket Tournament and enquired whether or not I could get complimentary admission tickets and autographs for them". Kalli provided complimentary tickets for all of us.

I was pleasantly surprised at the reception he got from several English youngsters- with their wholesome cockney accent,"Good afternoon, Mr. Kalli. Here for a game of cricket?" And did they mob him! Autographs again! A strategically placed phone call ensured I got admission to see West Indies Vs England at Lords.

With Pakistan tottering on the brink, their restless and despondent fans were clearly agitated, showering the West Indian fieldsmen with debris. Play resumed after Kalli approached the fans, and on bended knee appealed for calm. Shortly thereafter order was restored and in the process averting a potential confrontation which could have easily degenerated into something ugly.

Perhaps the greatest injustice done to Kalli was when some short- sighted, sanctimonious hypocrites banned him from West Indies cricket for being part of the rebel tour (along with 17 others) of then apartheid South Africa. The stench emanating from this sad, sorry saga continues to permeate the atmosphere. This blatant act to deprive these men from earning a living continues to be repugnant, reprehensible and unforgivable.

The "beautifully balanced, wristy batting star", by now a disillusioned man, signed to play for various clubs in South Africa, Australia and England. For Warwickshire he authored or co-authored several stupefying feats, becoming one of the more prolific scorers in English county cricket, with his best year being 1984 when he aggregated 2000 runs with 9 centuries.

He represented the W.I. in 66 tests, aggregating 4399 runs at an average of 44.43 with 12 centuries. The world class players at Lashings, a veritable who's who in cricket, deferentially refer to him as "the leg" (short for legend). He was Wisden Cricketer of the year in 1984.

Thank you Mr. Rudra Nath

By Abdool Ajib Karim

1959- Poverty was alive and doing extremely well in Port Mourant, Berbice, British Guiana.

To survive, our mothers and fathers had to toil in the sugar cane fields from early morning, while I twas still dark, and would return home late after sunset. Through heavy downpour and sicknesses, they trudged their way to work six days each week.

The children were left pretty much to fend for themselves. Our parents would leave us with strict instructions to perform an array of household chores. They would utter very stern warnings for us to go to school and be good. Our teachers knew that they have the blessings of our parents to punish us whenever necessary. However, the punishment could be excessive at times and sometimes not called for.

We devised highly imaginative ways to satisfy our hunger with a variety of fruits, fishes, birds and sugar cane. Those of us who were more daring escaped the maladies of malnutrition and scurvy.

I had just finished Primary School and had passed my School Leaving Examination. The results were published in the news papers. It was a very proud and important event in my life.

Chandisingh High School was the leading Secondary School within walking distance from my home. I wrote the entrance examination to that school, passed, and received a letter of acceptance for the new term commencing in September 1959.

As it turned out, my father fell ill and my chance to attend High School was dashed.

I then joined my cousin to fish in the savannahs, catching hassa, and selling them at the local market. I was pretty comfortable with my new life. This would have been my future with a possibility to be recruited into the sugar cane fields as a canecutter.

Then one evening, a little man, a stranger, showed up at our humble dwelling. He was accompanied by four respectable men from our neighborhood. Mr. Rudra Nath came into my life that day. He convinced my father not to worry about the school fees, but just to send me to school.

For years, when I reflect upon that moment, I just do not know how to express my undying gratitude to that little man, who changed my life and that of thousands of others -the vast majority of us poverty-stricken.

Mr. Nath devised every possible approach to change a "written in stone" age old tradition that followed us all the way from India to British Guiana. Our girl children were trained to focus and be accomplished on household chores, cooking, sewing and caring for babies, and anything else that may emerge along these lines. Parents were happy and pleased with themselves if they could find suitable husbands for their daughters, anywhere from the age of fourteen to sixteen years.

Rudra had one cry and one powerful message for all parents. Give the girls the same opportunity as the boys. Send them to High Schools and stop marrying them at such tender age. It was a hard sell, but many parents saw the wisdom of his message, and they complied.

And thanks to that message, five special girls came to Rose Hall High School--Joyce, Daro, Pamela, Sursati and Hemo. Today, after over forty-five years of marriage, five guys are still smiling happily Somanlall, Bansrajh, Ajib, Chandridat and the one and only Star (Ramesh).

I was fortunate, some years ago. Mr. Nath came to New York, a couple of months before he left us. He called me and we had a very long conversation. I thanked him profusely, and let him know that I am forever grateful to him for the future he had helped to fashion for me. I cannot comprehend what I would have been had he not come to our home that evening.

For me, High School days were the most memorable days of my life. I went to school with two friends, Bansrajh and Chandridat, with whom I shared the daily grind of poverty, which we forgot most of the times as we immersed ourselves in countless escapades. At school, we met Somanlall and Star, and eventually we became lifelong brothers.

We respected Mr. Nath, and we tried in so many ways to please him. When it came time to build the new Rose Hall High School in the reclaimed swamp area of Rose Hall, we volunteered for every project put forward. Somanlall and fellow student and friend, Nandlall, were involved heavily in all the constructions. We were right there besides them, and I must point out, that scores of other students participated and were equally enthusiastic about this project.

Then came the great rift between Mr. Nath and the Board of Governors.There were threats and rumors that the school would be torched. I remembered how we spent nights on the roof of the school, keeping watch, armed with pellet rifles. These memories are priceless.

We marched, demonstrated and won public support for our cause, but it was of no avail. We were compelled to evacuate the new school.

The open grandstands at the Port Mourant Race Course became our new classrooms in 1963.During break time; we would jog the entire circumference.

The majority of us were poor kids. It was a struggle to survive in our homes and environment. But those who had the power, never paused to consider the harm and injustice that they were perpetuating against a fragile group of students, who were seeking a way out.

With Mr. Nath and a staff of dedicated teachers leading on, a great majority of us passed the SeniorCambridge and GCE Examinations. It was the beginning of a new dawn for us.

SOMAN LALL

ACADEMIC JOURNEY AT RHS

Quotation of the day: Give a man a fish, you feed him for a day.

Teach a man to fish, you feed him for a lifetime.

This essence of education is found in the "Song of Guyana's Children":

"Born in the land of the Mighty Roraima,"

 Land of great rivers and far stretching sea;

So like the mountain, the sea and the river

Great wide and deep in our lives would we be.

Onward, upward may we ever go

Day by day in strength and beauty grow,

'Till at length we each of us will show

What Guyana sons and daughters can be."

One of the sons of Guyana was born on August 30, 1929 at Plantation Uitvlugt, in West Coast Demerara. He left the sugar estate in 1958 to fulfill his vision for education. He landed in the County of Berbice, where he established an Educational Institution in Rose Hall Village, now Rose Hall Town. With the aid and advice from prominent citizens of Albion Estate, Port Mourant Estate and Rose Hall Village areas, the School was named, "Rose Hall High School". And this son was no other than Rudra Nath.

In the latter part of 1959, I, enrolled with great anticipation at Rose Hall High School. Against the odds of age, distance and family requirements, I pursued with great expectations to be a successful student. And thereby, to have a very successful future.

Upon entering the door at Rose Hall High, I was greeted by Mr. A. K. Hari who directed me to the Principal's office and this was my first encounter with Mr. Nath. This meeting and his personality impacted me greatly.

I was placed in Form 2C where I met and interacted, very well with the students who were of my age group. They were very friendly and cooperative yet, very focused and serious about their education. After performing very well academically, I was awarded a scholarship which I maintained throughout my high school years.

I was promoted to Form 2A where I continued to progress academically. I then became a Prefect gaining the respect and admiration of my classmates and other students. During my scholastic years, the camaraderie that developed and existed was outstanding especially with dear friends like Bansraj Mangru, Chandradat Madho, Ajib Karim, Ronald Budhoo, Eva Bhairo, Yvonne Girdharry, Leon Maccoon, Dhanmattie Budhoo, Ronald Daly, Josephine Gilbert and so many others too numerous to name.

With admiration, love and respect, I pursued my education. My teachers had an outstanding influence over me and for a number of years they were my main source of information and inspiration which enabled me to develop better life skills and to have a better sense of direction about my life which helped to prepare me as a citizen of the world. At Rose Hall High School, I was not only being prepared for a job, but for Life.

The rise of the student population created the opportunity for a new school. We had to get a buiding large enough to accommodate the volume of students. A plot of land was acquired partly through donation and partly through purchase. Mr. Nath, together with the approval of the other members of the Board of Governors, embarked on a mission of fund raising, donation and volunteering to erect this new school. Mr. Cecil Ramoo, a construction contractor supplied the work force for the building and the supervision of the student volunteers. I took a leadership role with the other students during the project and with a lot of hard work the mission was successfully accomplished.

Things went well until Mr. Nath and the Board of Governors began to disagree on matters of administration and financing. Unfortunately, Mr. Nath was served with a legal writ restraining him from entering the school compound. For me, personally, this was traumatic and a sad experience. Our Principal, who was now an icon to his students, was being asked to vacate the very project that he envisioned for his students' future. This very project was his "brainchild". Parents were advised of the departure from the school.

With the aid of Haman Ben Yassin and a written permit from the Police Department I led the whole student body out of Rose Hall High School (Reef). Mr. Nath, at this point contacted Mr. Rahaman, who kindly donated the building at Port Mourant Race Tract to be our temporary place of learning. In a few months, we merged with Port Mourant Comprehensive Institute which gave rise to the new name of Corentyne Comprehensive High School. An additional building was erected to help house the volume of students.

I continued my role, as Head Prefect and dedicated student, by which I was honored with a Plaque of Recognition for the afore-mentioned. Upon my success at the General Certificate of Education, I became a teacher. I followed the examples of my principal and former educators and continued in the promotion of Education.

In retrospect, I reveled in the fact that, I was very active and dedicated in the construction and establishment of RHS which is now Lower Corentyne Secondary, and CCHS, which is still a Shining Star in the Port Mourant District. My encouragement came primarily, from my Principal and the dedicated Teachers. I was encouraged during my student days, by none other than Prema Sukra also know as, Parasram Balkissoon who provided, through his parents, accommodation and friendly boyhood nurturing. I congratulate all the students who went through enormous strains moving from building to building, and yet, still achieved academic successes.

My greatest thanks to our Icon, Mr. Rudra Nath and his dedicated and knowledgeable staff for the wonderful jobs they executed. We, the students, looked back, in awe and are proud of our achievements and our current role in today's society. I now end with a heartfelt Quote from Mr. Nath:

"We all have the God-given abilities to do anything we truly wish to do. Those simple farmers and plantation workers and their children, together with the merchants and professionals of our Berbice community achieved more than any other community I know of in Guyana in the field of Education".

Roopan Kuldip

I started my high school in 1965 after a season of cutting rice. My loving mother took me to Rose Hall high School at the water-side (Reef). My first form was 2A Sanichar. I worked very hard. I spent one term in form 2 before going to form 3. The teachers were all very helpful and encouraging and they inspired me to work hard. This work ethic was instilled in me to work very hard for everything. I finished high school with seven subjects. I was a teacher at Helena Gov't school in Mahaica. I ended up in Montreal where I graduated from Concordia University and eventually a chartered accountant. I believe that my academic success was due to the encouragement I received during my fabulous high school days.

Highlights at Comprehensive

It is only after I left high school that I look back and cherish those wonderful and memorable High school days.

Each student thinks that his/ her final year was the best but I felt that mine was the best because of the following:

Our form was 5A Ramkerrat, the only Latin form. Ramkerrat

was our math teacher with fair complexion. We had a great mixture of students in our form. Rarnkerrat left a great impression on me. I started at Rose Hall high school at the water side (Reef), then had to move to Port Mourant Race Course Pavillion and then to CCHS..

I had the pleasure of knowing many teachers like Sanichar, Hari, Ralph etc. They all left an indelible impression on me. I am still in contact with some of my fellow teachers and classmates.

I have a passion for learning, a passion that was instilled in me because of some of the great people I was fortunate to have met during my high school days. I myself became a teacher because of that experience. I was a teacher at Helena Gov't School at Mahaica.I then migrated to New York, where I spent two years working. I then came to Montreal, Canada. I have been here for over forty years. I am presently a Chartered Accountant.

REFLECTIONS OF A NATIVE SON

ROSE HALL HIGH SCHOOL: A SELF-HELP SUCCESS

BY MILTON LATCHA

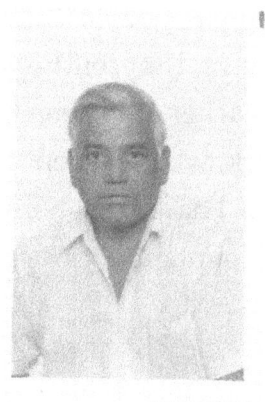

As the decade of the '50s came to a close, the people of Rose Hall decided that the time had come to fill a void that had long existed in their community. For local teenagers and young adults who were either too poor or too old to gain admission to any of our existing secondary schools, there were literally no educational alternatives. So the community came together to create an alternative of its own: a local high school open to anyone with a willingness to learn regardless of age or record of prior academic accomplishment. Students would be enrolled in classes commensurate with their capabilities and permitted to remain for as long as they possessed the desire to work hard, master the curriculum and advance at their own pace.

It was a plan as audacious as it was unprecedented. Indeed, the construction of Rose Hall High School more than half a century ago might be considered the most successful project of its kind undertaken at that time. It was a triumph of bold and innovative leadership, supported by a dedicated following of teachers, students and a highly motivated community galvanized by a shared vision of collective empowerment.

The school itself has been a boon to generations of students who had yearned for a quality secondary education but were unable to gain admission to other established high schools in the area. For many, it was not for lack of academic ability that they were excluded, but because of their age or, to a lesser extent, their modest financial circumstances.

But Rose Hall High School did not discriminate; its doors were open to students of all ages for as long as they were willing to learn. Some have likened its impact in the community to the biblical Parting of the Red Sea on the march to educational freedom. The school was a resounding success, with teachers and students alike performing admirably -- and often with distinction – in academia, sports and community service. The people of Rose Hall and nearby villages supported the cause wholeheartedly – through periods of smooth sailing and periods of rough sailing. Theirs was a remarkable, exemplary and mutually beneficial collaboration between the community and the institution it founded to serve a public need and promote the public good.

Looking back now on my experience as a teacher at the school during its formative years, I am reminded of the hope I expressed at the end of my speech on opening day: that Rose Hall High School as the ship, Mr. Rudra Nath as the captain, our fellow teachers as the crew and our students as the passengers we will sail the seas of ambition to arrive at the shore of success."

This we did.

BHARRAT LATCHMAN

Before   After

As a little boy growing up in "Bound-yard", one of the most poverty stricken and economically backward areas of the sugar plantation of Port Mourant, life was terrible. Surviving from day to day was extremely difficult for us, a family of 10 living on very meager earnings and in over-crowded living quarters. In the deplorable health, social and economic conditions that plagued the inhabitants of "Bound-yard", a high school education was beyond the means of most -- Once you were born in that cycle of poverty, there was little prospect of getting anywhere. Education was the key to getting out and up. But that was only within the reach of the privileged few with the financial means. I was not one among them.

"Bound-yard" was a somewhat remote, low-lying area of the sugar plantation, Port Mourant, where the indentured plantation labourers from India were initially housed in rows of little shacks or "joined-up cottages" no bigger than 10 feet by 10 feet per family. I vividly remember, every time there was a period of heavy rain (which was quite often) the entire area of "bound-yard" would be flooded and we would be walking barefooted in knee-deep dirty and germ infested flood waters. During one such flood, while walking home bare foot from school, I stepped on a broken bottle and I had my small right toe almost completely severed. That incident had been etched in my memory every since as the mark of that injury is still with me. And Oh yes! Whenever there was a rain fall, the zinc roof of our little cottage would leak. We usually had to catch the rain fall coming through the tiny holes of the roof with a bucket or a bowl.

Life in "Bound-yard" was particularly terrible for us being a family of ten. Imagine a family of 10 crammed in a 10 feet by 10 feet shack. We each slept on one jute rice bag spread on the wooden floor lying side-by-side. Lying so closely adjacent to each other, there was little or no room between us to lay our hands. As a result, some of us had to keep our arms above our heads for most of the night.

I was the third child of a family of seven brothers and three sisters. My father and mother were both labourers in the sugar plantation. The meagre earnings from their hard labour were often insufficient to feed and clothed our large family. Paying for a high school education was absolutely out of our reach. This situation became even worst when the sugar factory was closed by the British owners to penalize the people of Port Mourant for their strong support of the late Dr. Cheddie Jagan, former President of Guyana, who was at the time trying to secure British Guiana's (now Guyana) independence from the British colonial rulers. With the closing of the sugar factory, both of my parents became unemployed and they began struggling to earn a living from cultivating a small plot of rice land given to us by one of my aunts, a little vegetable garden and catching fish and selling in the local markets.

Faced with such difficult living conditions, I could not even dream of going to a high school so immediately after graduating from elementary school I joined my parents and other brothers, helping in the rice cultivation, vegetable garden, and fishing almost daily, and oh, take care of the one cow that we keep for the milk. I remember having to walk barefoot 20 to 25 miles a day to the far ends of the sugar cane and rice fields to catch fish and bring back on time for my mother to sell at the Port Mourant market.

I attended St. Joseph's Anglican School. After completing my elementary school education in 1958, I stayed home for over a year helping my parents. My father always believed that education was the best thing a parent could give his children. He often told us that no matter how much money or other material things you have, those things could always be taken away from you but education is the one thing that no one can take away from you. He was always on the lookout for any opportunity to send me to high school. At one point my father explored the possibility of sending me to Chandisingh (Corentyne) High School. Unfortunately, my parents could not afford the fees.

About a year had passed since completing elementary school, and I was still engaged in fishing, gardening and rice cultivation. At this point, I was beginning to lose all hope of ever getting a high school education. But miracles do happen. One day while I was fishing with my father, a gentleman mentioned to him that a new high school was opened up at Rose Hall Village – Rock Diamond Hotel and that the Principal, Mr. Rudra Nath was a very good man and would accept whatever little fees students could afford. My father took his advice and we went to see the principal, Mr. Rudra Nath. That day began the educational journey that took me through the crowded, often hot and uncomfortable classrooms at Rock Diamond Hotel to the lecture halls of Canadian universities and to the comfortable offices and boardrooms of the Government of Ontario.

I began attending Rose Hall High School (RHS) at Rock Diamond Hotel in 1960. I was placed in Form one which was on the ground floor. While there, on a number of occasions I joined other students, teachers, parents and volunteers to help with the construction of the new school at the swamp section of Rose Hall Village. I really admired the dedication and hard work of the many students and teachers who assisted with the construction of the new school. I remember when we moved from Rock Diamond hotel to the new building, it was still under construction. The building was not completely enclosed, the concrete wall was only about waist high, without windows, and often a beautiful sea breeze would blow right across our class.

After a short stay in Form I at Rock Diamond, I was placed in Form II in the new building. I did not fully completed form II before I was again promoted to Form IV. Advancing students from one grade to the next higher grade level in quick succession was called "accelerated promotion". While this meant fewer years in school, less tuition fees to pay and getting quicker to writing the final exams (GCE and Senior Cambridge) - two years instead of three or more years - it also meant much, much, harder and longer hours of study, burning the kerosine hand lamp well past mid-night. I had no clock or radio at home. So I never knew what time I went to bed after studying late in the night. Usually, I would go to bed when the oil in the hand lamp had burned out or the shade had become so dark that I could no longer read.

In 1963, I had just completed about two years at Rose Hall High School, when we began final preparation for the GCE exam. But before completing our preparation for the GCE exam, the students and teachers were forced to move to the Port Mourant race course pavilion due to the dispute between the Principal, Mr. Rudra Nath and the Board of Directors. That is where I spent the final month preparing for the GCE Exam. Despite these challenges and setbacks, I wrote the GCE and Senior Cambridge exams and I did well in both.

In 1963, I began teaching at an elementary school in Black Bush Polder. There I met my beautiful wife. We have been blessed with a lovely daughter and a wonderful son, both graduates of the University of Toronto. We also have a wonderful and loving grand-daughter.

While teaching, I studied privately on my own and passed 4 GCE "A" level subjects. In 1968, I began teaching at Corentyne High School. This was a rather gratifying experience for me as this was the very high school I could not attend because my parents could not afford the fees.

In 1970, I left Guyana to pursue studies in Canada. After completing graduate studies at Queen's University, in Ontario, Canada, I got a teaching job at the same university in 1974. This continued my teaching career, which began at the elementary school level, then to the secondary school level and on to the university level. While teaching at Queen's University, I was offered a teaching position at the University of Guyana, but after careful deliberations I decided against it.

In 1980, I decided to try a different occupation and took a job as manager of the research department of a major labour union. I worked there until 1990 when I again decided it was time to experience working in another field. So I joined the Government of Ontario where I worked as a Senior Economist until my retirement on April 30, 2013.

I must say that whatever humble achievements I experienced during this journey are due firstly to the enormous sacrifice, dedication, undying determination and hard work of my beloved parents. I shall remain forever grateful to them.

And secondly, to the Principal of RHS, the late Mr. Rudra Nath, a true visionary, and a dedicated educator, who opened the door, provided the opportunities and made it possible for me and many others who attended RHS to afford a high school education. Mr. Nath and his group of dedicated and committed teachers provided us with the teachings, guidance and knowledge that lay the foundation and set us on the path and journey to higher education and greater achievements. I am truly thankful to them.

A special Thanks to Mr. Adarsh Hari for providing this opportunity to review our special memories.

CHATTERDEI IRIS BRIJPAUL NEE MANGAL

Before   After

In late 1958, Mr Nath, a visionary and a few faithful teachers founded the Rose Hall High School. The classes were held at what was then called the Rock Diamond Hotel. Young men and especially women who would have literally fallen by the wayside were given a chance to get a high school education. Many went on to excel in different fields. My older brother was given that chance.

In 1960, I did not succeed at the Pupil Teachers Examination at Albion Canadian Mission School. I had another chance to redo the exam, so I was going back to school to do just that. If I failed the second time around, then educationally all doors would be closed for me. My older sister and our friends were having arranged marriages at the tender age of fourteen and fifteen. This would have been the path for me as well; it was the norm in those days. My future looked bleak as my parents could not afford to pay tuition fees for another child to attend high school. I needed a miracle.

In those days, there were hardly any forms of exposure to the public media. My parents were uneducated and none of us understood that investing in a girl's education would eventually benefit the family, the community and the whole of society for generations to come. Mr.

Nath knew this and empowered a group of young people to take charge and change their destiny.

My prayers for a miracle came through. Lady Luck was smiling on me. My older brother got apprenticed at the Port Mourant Training school and he would receive a stipend of six dollars per week. That created an opening for me. Also an uncle of mine encouraged my parents to give me the chance at high school, he promised to help with the fees "now and then".

That September of 1960, a hopeful, nervous, maybe excited newly clad and shod fourteen-year old with a dollar spending money and her school fees in her pocket ventured to high school. I got the chance of a lifetime to prove myself, to make a difference in my life and to make my parents proud.

The mode of travelling at that time was a half an hour walk to the main public road to join a bus or taxi for a twenty minutes ride to school. The cost per trip was five cents. Later my parents would buy me a bicycle. I will not mention the numerous times I fell off that bike or how difficult it was to pedal against the wind. I survived it all; my friend and riding companion sadly did not.

Looking back now, everything seemed to be fast forwarded, new and difficult lessons were learnt, homework and studies had to be completed, new and lasting friendships were forged and there were always the never ending chores at home. On a lighter note, I found geometry to be too abstract for me; I understood the concepts of the theorems, did the proofs correctly, but found it difficult to figure out why a straight line had to stand on another straight line. It took me a while to fathom that; I still laugh at myself. My teachers were dedicated and encouraging, always pointing the way to success. The four years flew by, but not without difficulty and insecurity; I had to change school buildings and locations four times. This was probably a blessing in disguise; I was being prepared for the semi nomadic life I would live for the next twenty-five years.

I graduated from high school in 1964 and got a teaching job away from home. I was eighteen years old with a dream and a prayer in my heart. I was heading into the unknown. As fate would have it, I met my future husband and we got married in 1966.The children came along, two daughters first and then two sons. In between raising my children and working, it was necessary for me to do teachers' training for a secure job position and for seniority. I enrolled at the Teachers' Training College for the In-Service Training program which would take me two years of evening classes for completion. I graduated in 1973.

Even though teaching is a better profession for a woman raising a family, because of the long summer vacations; it was getting difficult for me to keep up with all my responsibilities. I made the decision to be a stay- at- home mom. Even though I would sometimes complain about "cooking and washing my life away", I did not remain stagnant, I kept reading, learning and travelling with my children and husband. Education was our first priority at home. One by one, my children did under and post graduate studies and then they flew the nest. They are now making their contribution to society. I am a proud grandma of five beautiful grandchildren and number six will soon be here.

When I was approached to write this article, I had second thoughts, I did not consider myself successful in any way as I did not accomplish any higher studies nor did I climb any corporate ladder. I was just a "lowly" stay- at- home mom. As I began to reminisce and write, however, my life experiences fell into perspective. I enjoyed a meaningful life. Today on the eve of my 66th birthday, I am living my best life ever. I am forever grateful to my God and the Universe for giving me that balance, to my parents and teachers for their guidance, to my family and friends for their constant support in my life's journey.

BANSRAJ MANGRU AND ANJANIE MANGRU

Before   After   Anjanie

It is with great pleasure and it is very refreshing to share my great memories. I, Bansraj Mangroo, the class of 1963- 1964, was born at Ankerville, Port Mourant. I attended St. Joseph Anglican primary school.

For my secondary education, time was hard, and it seemed impossible to further my education. We were four brothers and two sisters and my parents found it difficult to make ends meet. Thanks to Rudra Nath, Principal of Rose Hall high school, who gave me the opportunity to further my education. I was not qualified to attend Chandi Singh High school.

Rudra Nath and the teachers opened the doors for the unfortunate by going to people's homes and advising parents to send their children to Rose Hall high school. Rock Diamond Hotel had two stories. We were occupying the top floor. With this support from the public with parents sending their children to our school we were getting overcrowded with students coming from all over Corentyne Berbice.

Rudra decided to construct our new school building in the reef section of Rose Hall Village. Lots of help was given. Help came from teachers, students, parents, volunteers, contractors and carpenters. Noor Mohamed volunteered his help in carpentry. Cement was given by Ramjeet Construction and others. The student body comprised of so many boys and girls were headed by Somanlall and Nandlall in all phases of construction on the building. We worked hard to raise money. Concerts and planned events were performed as well as monetary collections from house to house. It took a long time but finally Rose Hall High School was completed.

The education system used by Rudra and teachers was well organized with fruitful results. The atmosphere within the school system was pleasant amongst the students and teachers. Then, Rudra formed the Board of Governors and then trouble started with the final outcome Rudra was asked to resign as principal. Rudra was dedicated to the students and the students supported him in all protests marching on the road and doing things to preserve our high school. Finally, the Board of Governors got a court order banning Rudra from entering the premises of Rose Hall High School. It was about the same time we were scheduled to write the London, GCE 'O' level Examination.

Seeing there was a huge problem between Rudra and the Board of Governors, Rudra decided to move RHS to the Port Mourant Race Course. The race course was three flights high and it was arranged in such a way to accommodate the students by sectioning it into forms (classrooms). The arrangement was well organized. During that time, the results from the London GCE 'O' level were received. Our results were very good. We were even considered to have had better results (more distinctions) than Chandi Singh High School, our competitor.

Our school days were full of fun and excitement. We were very committed to our educational pursuits. However, love, courtship and infatuation were also a life's game. We were three friends known as the ABC from primary school until today. A-Abdool Ajib Karim; B-Bansraj Mangroo and C-Chandradutt Madho Persaud. While attending Rose Hall High School we had two other buddies, Somanlall and Ramesh Chand Jagroo and we were all very close and this friendship still stands very strong even today-- the beauty of love and friendship. Ajib married Pamela Bachan; Bansraj married Anjanie Mangroo; Chandradat married Chandrawattie Kissoon; Somanlall married Sursattie Ramdhanny and Ramesh maried Hemwattie Jagmohan.

After graduation from high school I migrated to the United States and worked as a medical laboratory technologist at the State University of New York, Downstate Medical Center then later became laboratory technologist supervisor. Then at Long Island College Hospital I was a Hematology Technologist.I was also a laboratory technologist at the Kings County Hospital, Dekab Community Hospital, St. Mary's Hospital and Jamaica Hospital. I was the Union Representative for the State University of New York/ United University Professions.

After retiring from the medical profession in New York, my wife and I relocated to Florida and opened La Price West Indian Groceries at 2101 West Chesnut Street, Tampa. My wife and I also host the Geet Mala TV Show shown on Time Warner, Channel 44 on Sunday,10 :30 a.m and the Geet Mala Radio Show on WQBN 1300 A.M every Sunday from 6 PM to 7 PM.

LEILA MANGRU APRIL 30, 2012

WHEN NIGHTS WERE DARK AND DAYS WERE LONG

And the tunnel of hoplessness seemed infinite

And the kiskadee cries were the cries of a soul

Seeking answers in the dark that light may descend

The answers came in the form of a hope and a vision!

My great hope – as seen through the walls of my high school – was to have the vision that could somehow break the cycle of suffering and struggle I experienced through my parents lives and the lives of those about me.

What are the significant experiences of this soul's academic journey through the halls of RHS, PMCI and CC HS? They are the experiences of visionaries who knew not what they were but who by their lives and hearts gave us a vision of endless possibilities of what we may become.

So let me backtrack a little for no journey occurs alone. The year is 1959. My mother, who was not expected to survive, had just given birth to my eighth sibling. As the eldest daughter (one older brother, Jagat James) I was called out of 6th standard at St. Joseph's Anglican School one sunny day and asked to go on home.

There were meals to cook, shopping to do, children to feed and bathe, a house to clean and saucepans to be ready for my father to catch the sugar estate bus at 5 a.m. to go to work.

Needless to say the future looked grim and every breath was a prayer to the One who must have some answers hidden somewhere within. In due time, much to my joy, my mother slowly recovered and I went on my knees before my father and asked if I may go to high school.

So in 1962 way too old and poor for Corentyne High School, my mother accompanied this scared, half blind and hopeful one to the swamplands of Rose Hall where a gleaming L-shape building glistened in the middle of seemingly nowhere.

Here I got to know Miss Prema, a sweet bespectacled woman who registered me and sent me on to a Mr. Birbahadur who was to be my Form Two master and Geography teacher. One incident that struck my young heart was the sense of compassion, respect, and dignity my form master and all my classmates demonstrated in handling the following situation.

One of the young ladies being called to the chalkboard was discovered to have her period. A silent gasp and hush fell on the class. Oh God! What next? Then our visionary form master nodded to two young ladies to flank the young lady and accompany her to the office where Miss Prema and Miss Shirinarine, visionaries among women, made everything seemed normal, kept our psyche intact, and taught us invaluable lessons of compassion, understanding, acceptance and helpfulness. At that moment I also knew that I was safe, was among people I could trust, and blossomed from a scared kid to become the speaker to eulogize John F. Kennedy on his assassination, a class prefect and later a school prefect. I owe all I am able to accomplish to all those dear, precious souls, my teachers who believed in me and encouraged me to study that "I can do it".

Mr. Ruda Nath, founder and principal of RHS and CCHS, was a visionary person who showed love, compassion and understanding to all irrespective of status, financial situation, color or creed. Though small in stature, he lived and taught Universal love and the brotherhood and oneness of all. I marveled at his seemingly ability to 'materialize' out of nowhere, once he found me, when I was carrying on a long conversation with a male teacher, "Liloutie", he scolded softly, "you must so live as to not give a wrong impression of what you are not. Now you get home and help your parents." And he waved me off on my Raleigh bicycle while he continued to patrol the school grounds for tardy ones. It was my humble privilege to continue learning from him until two weeks before his passing. And I say of him as I said of Gandhi "Today the light went out of..... In days to come men shall wonder if such a one actually walked this earth."

It is because of the encouragement and trust of mentors and teachers like Ramkisson, Madray, Asregaddo, Jaggarnauth, Hari, Sanichar, Chando, Birbahadur, Rawana and Misses Shrinarine and Prema that made it possible for me to write and pass six GCE's less than three years after commencing high school.

From this beginning all doors to further education were open. I came on a student visa to Mankato State University in Minnesota, then to University of Iowa. After graduating with a Masters degree my husband and I, with our two sons, age 3 and 2 months old, left the United States to teach in Jamaica; later in Kenya, and then in North Dakota, where I spent the first two years at home and at the university library to complete my Doctorate from California Coast University. As soon as I graduated with my doctorate the university hired me to be the Director for the center for Multicultural Affairs. A car accident in 2003 ended a rewarding professional life, so I stayed home as a volunteer to tutor international students with their English and to help some in making the necessary adjustments for university life and a new environment

In 2009, we retire near an organic farm and meditation center in Live Oak, Florida, where we volunteer as cooks, gardeners. Other times are spent in volunteer tutoring (mostly migrants), meditation, travelling, being with family and friends and just giving thanks for all the people who touched our lives and made us richer than they would ever realize. Thank you each one for making so much possible and for helping to fulfill a vision and a hope!!!!!!

RUDRA NATH:

PORTRAIT OF A PRINCIPAL, PATRIOT AND POLITICIAN--

HIS LIFE'S WORK SHOULD BE HONORED

MOSES NAGAMOOTOO

I received a terse email: *"Mr. Rudra Nath died in Florida."* It was from an old student of Corentyne Comprehensive High School, where I taught when Rudra Nath was the Principal.

Since then, my mind has been traveling back in time, reviewing when and how I knew Rudra Nath, reflecting on his pioneering work as an educationist, the years we shared together as political activists and how his philosophy of life influenced me. When the news of Rudra Nath's death reached me as I was about to travel for the United States, I promised myself that as soon as I could do so, I would write a tribute to his work and memory. However, in New

York I was invited to meet socially with a Guyanese gathering and I grabbed the opportunity to talk about the life and example of Rudra Nath.

Two coincidences stood out at that meeting: firstly, the organizer was Joe Kanhai, who was introduced to me by Rudra Nath sometime in 1963 as a PPP militant from Port Mourant; and secondly, Mr. Persaud, a former headmaster, reminded me that Rudra Nath was born at Uitvlugt but later moved to his home village of Vergenoegen on the West Coast of Demerara. Rudra, he disclosed, had started his career as a bicycles repairman.

How did he come to the Corentyne? That is a long and interesting story, the exact beginning I do not know first-hand. I learned that he and his parents re-located in Rose Hall sometime in 1959 or there about, and that Rudra Nath had opened a high school in an unlikely building I knew only as "Rock Diamond", formerly a hotel. Soon after, he started a public campaign to build a school in the swampy, crab-grass area close to the Rose Hall reef or foreshore, to be known as Rose Hall High School.

ROSE HALL SWAMP

I enrolled at that "swamp" school in September 1962 when the building was still under construction and students were giving voluntary labour towards its completion. I still picture senior students like Baythoo Nandalall, Soman Lall and Premchand Dass pushing around wheel-barrows and fetching buckets of sand and cement at the site. I remember meeting Mr. Nath in the unfinished staff room, and asking him to admit me as I had made much sacrifice to get $18 for the first term's fees. Fees, he retorted, were not important. What was important to him, he added softly, is that the children of the poor should have an education, and that he would make sure that they do, at least in the Berbice area. Those words were to be, since then, a source of great inspiration to me in all that I did and was to become.

Rudra Nath kept faith with his promise. After my first term he gave me "accelerated promotion" from the second to the fourth form, and six months later he posted me to the fifth form, with the "big league" then preparing for the General Certificate of Education (London) examinations.

Rudra Nath was out to promote talent when he recognized it in any student. He had boasted excellent results in previous exams at the Senior Cambridge levels in students like Miss Rai, Hardutt Punwassie, Mohanlall Birbahadur, Basil Jaggernath and Mahadeo Rajdhanny, to name only a few "A" students. Nath's "swamp" school was rivaling the long-established Corentyne High School.

He had good teachers, all dedicated to Nath's purpose. Among the early ones were Yassin Sankar and Yassin Ben, both of whom taught Literature; William Rawana, my Latin master; Vernon Asregadoo, as well as Ramkissoon, Ramnarine and Ramkeerat (we used to pronounce the first syllable in the last three names,"Rum"), Hariprashad, Chando Narine, Miss Prema, Naidu, Hari and Sanichar. Sooner, he added a team of his "A" students to his staff of competent teachers. By June 1964 I was writing GCE and, before results were out, Rudra Nath appointed me a junior English teacher.

STRIVE FOR EXCELLENCE

If Rudra Nath's politics were Gandhian non-violence, his philosophy on education was that of Rabindranath Tagore. He felt that one should strive for excellence even if one were to be educated under a tree. So it was not surprising that Nath's school became a melting pot of talent from children who were born and raised literally in the cane and rice fields.

It was Nath's school that incubated singers like Roopdai, Etwaroo and Tajewattie Singh; first-class athletes like Alvin Kallicharran (cricket) and Anand Sookram (table tennis). It was at that school that I was to make acquaintance with Premchand Dass and Michael Dutchin, who were to become forefront PPP activists for Guyana's independence and later, the restoration of democracy. But Nath's idealism and altruism were not shared by every one. Whilst I was in Form 4 his Board of Governors threw Nath out of the school he had built. When he walked, he took with him all of his students and re-started school at the Port Mourant Race Course. We were huddled in several forms in the two grand pavilions and, as my memory raced back to that time, I can still smell the dust, stale dung, and the dank sweat of horses, as I did while being prepared for exams in the "stables". Nath later moved his students to the old Port Mourant factory compound, where there was an existing school, and merged to form what is today the Corentyne Comprehensive High School.

Rudra Nath was an exceptionally determined person. I remember him traveling around on bicycle, then on motor-cycle and later in a "match-box" Volkswagon carrying the message that children of the poor must have an education. His fees were small, and his encouragement was always great. He organized countrywide fundraisers for his school building project. As a student, I was given my first break on stage when I played my own guitar and sang calypsoes and country western at the fundraisers. I began teaching at the Corentyne Comprehensive High School.

Rudra was also a great disciplinarian. I vividly remember when someone threw a bench at a teacher, while his back was turned to the blackboard. No one would confess. So Rudra summoned his beloved nephew, who was living with him at the time. He pulled him over the bench and gave him six lashes with a cane. Nath broke the cane thereafter, and he was almost in tears as he told us this story: a boy was walking on the road; he saw a piece of wood with a nail sticking out from it. He stepped on the wood, and his foot was pierced. Another boy was also walking on the road; he did not see the nail on the wood, but stepped on it, and was pierced. "What was common is that whether one does something by accident or by design, one feels the pain." His nephew had to feel pain by accident or design in not disclosing who threw the bench at the teacher.

TREMENDOUS RESPECT

I did not see Rudra very much after 1973 or so. He visited me at my house in Georgetown sometime in 2000 when I was still a Government Minister. When I saw him I ran as quickly as I could, bare-footed and in shorts, to open the gate for my old headmaster and mentor. Over tea at my bottom-house, he told me of his plan to build a college in Berbice. I promised to help in whatever ways I could. I volunteered to contact Punwassie, an old student/teacher who had become a successful engineer, about designing the edifice and supervising its construction. I assured him that "B", as he knew Punwassie, would gladly do this for him free of cost!

As he was leaving he told me that he was proud that I had remained at the side of Cheddi Jagan, and had seen the struggle through to victory. He looked at my bare feet, and he said: "You didn't have to open the gate for me." He smiled, still looking down, and added: "But, then, I am not disappointed. It's good to know that you remain humble as I have taught my students to be."

Rudra Nath was also at Cheddi's side, for many years. In 1964 he was the Chairman of the No 3 Constituency (Dr. Jagan's area) spanning Port Mourant to Black Bush Polder. I was to succeed him in that position the following year, which he didn't take kindly, but we worked together for the party tooth and nail, and he was seen as the guru in our circle comprising Pandit Tiwari, Sydney Joseph, Hazrat Insanally, Joe Kanhai, Dandy Baichan, Beckles, Paloo and others.

He did a lot more that earned him tremendous respect. His presence anywhere commanded attention. Once, when Dara Singh, the Indian wrestler and actor, came to Guyana for exhibition bouts, there was a near riot at the Port Mourant cricket ground. There were so many people all crashing against the fence that separated them from the wrestling ring that the stage almost collapsed. The agitated crowd would listen to no one. Then the just-above-five feet, diminutive, bespectacled Rudra Nath stepped on the stage. In a soft voice, he asked for calm and for reason, and he got it.

His politics apart, Rudra Nath's greatest achievements were his pioneering work as an educationist, which must not be forgotten. For a start, I believe consideration ought to be given to rename a suitable school in his honor, the *"Rudra Nath Memorial High".*

(The writer, a former student and teacher at the high school founded by Rudra Nath, was a Government Minister and is presently a Member of Parliament and an Attorney)

PARASAR NANDAN

MY EDUCATIONAL JOURNEY AT RHS

My name is Parasar Nandan, born on the 31st August at 3.30 a.m at Number 27 Bush Lot Village, with a population of 300. The villagers were mostly farmers engaged in the cultivation of rice, green vegetables, rearing of cattle and livestock and poultry. However, there were a few who engaged in trades such as carpentry, painting and other skillful occupation.

I attended a nursery school housed in a dilapidated wooden building in the village. It was run by Mrs. Lyte, a middle aged lady, who lived in the neighboring village. From this school, all the children who spent nine months to one year were enrolled at The Kildonan Church of Scotland School at Nurney Village. It was September 1947 and I spent my entire Primary School years at this location. In 1957 I wrote the Primary School Certificate Examination.

While I was at primary school, my father, who was ailing for sometime, passed away leaving my brother of three years old and I, to be taken care of by my mother. My four older sisters were already married so there was a great responsibility on my mother to care for us both, financially. I was now sixteen years old and my help to home was invaluable. I never entertain the thought that I would ever attend high school because my younger brother was only thirteen and I wanted him to have both primary and secondary education. Sad to say, he was truant and it was difficult for him to attend school.

By this time Sept. 1958. a new school was established at Rose Hall Village, about 7/1/2 miles from where I lived. I did not pay much attention to the opening of this school for the following reasons. One was my age and the other was our economic situation. We were poor and without my help at home, we were in dire financial situation.

Around November 1958, I noticed that a few boys from my village were attending the new school. I became curious and learnt that students of any age were admitted. I gained my mother's permission and she accompanied me to enroll. I became a student on January 26,1959 and was placed in Form 2. The building, housing the new school, was the former Rock Diamond Hotel. It was built for a purpose other than a school. That business was no longer thriving and it was sold to a local businessman who eventually rented the premises to Mr. Rudra Nath for the purpose of establishing the school. "THAT BUILDING BECAME OUR SCHOOL".

My first day was strangely exciting because of the new enrollment and my new classmates. The boys were dressed in blue shirts and Khaki pants and the girls in white blouses and green skirts. This was very impressionable and I looked forward to being a student. Shortly after, there were two more admissions, William Ramcharran and Victor Bertle who became my closest friends. We three, were placed on a bench made for two. We were one term behind the current Form 2. Most of the students in this form were successful at the Primary School Certificate Examination

I observed that there were only three forms and three teachers, who were the Principal, Mr. Rudra Nath, Mr. Udai Panday and the very young Adarsh K. Hari. We were taught all the subjects that were on a High School agenda, including Hindi and excluding Science. The term rolled along smoothly, enrollments were increasing and the classrooms were now over populated. There were need for more teachers and restructuring of the classes. We wrote the annual examination in July, 1959 and most of the students were successful and were promoted to Form 3 A. About fifteen students were selected and given accelerated promotion to Form 4B. Together with Form 4 A, we began preparation to write the College of Preceptors Examination which resulted in a success of 90 percent. It was very hard work for the students with accelerated promotion but they met the challenge. Without this school we, the over-aged students, would not have had an opportunity for a secondary education.

At this point, the following teachers were added to the staff: Dr. Jack Banergie, who came from West Demerara but left after a term; Mr. Vernon Asregadoo, Mr. Raymond Singh and Ms. Hanna Prema. There were others that joined the staff as time progressed. These young teachers worked diligently and their efforts paid off handsomely. We were then being groomed to write the joint Oxford and Cambridge Examination in 1961. The school encountered a snag. Registration was not accepted on the grounds that the students would not have completed the required four-year course, Mr. Nath provided validity because most of the students to be registered had attended a secondary school and were transferred to RHS. Registration was granted and the students were able to write their exam with acceptable results, and, "FLYING COLORS", if I may add.

After Senior Cambridge, I went back to school in order to achieve a credit in English. I was successful and received duplicated credits in other subjects. I entered the teaching profession and after working at several schools I ended up at Yakusari Primary as the Head Master. My tenure as a teacher and Head Master totaled thirty-two and a half years. In March 1995 I migrated to the United States, and, after six years working, I accepted a sponsorship to Canada.

I would like to relate an unpleasant incident while in school. I was unsuccessful in dissuading my friend from not paying his school fees. We eventually teamed up as a group of thirteen and went to Auntie Betty's Spirit Shop. We were in the midst of enjoying our doses of alcoholic beverages when suddenly Mr. Haman Ben Yassim appeared. He asked for a cigarette and we were very hesitant and unsure of his motive. We asked him under what capacity he came, whether to join us or to report us to the Assistant Principal. He did not answer and retreated back to school. We continued imbibing to our hearts' content and went home.

I arrived at school the next morning to a reception line in front of Mr. Nath's office. All my cohorts were being accosted by Mr. Nath and I saw the gloom on their faces. A member of the Board of Governors addressed us, and I, not knowing who he was, I rudely said, "who the hell are you"? Without waiting for an answer. I broke ranks and walked out. Expulsion was threatened but after the regular parental involvement, we were re-accepted in school.

Thanks to Mr. Nath and his team of teachers, who came at the most opportune time, to enable us, the over aged students to accomplish a secondary education and secure our places both in Guyana and internationally. A very good job, indeed, Mr. Nath. THANK YOU!

RUDRA NATH BY JULIUS NATHOO

My acquaintance with Rudra Nath was brief when compared to other school principals with whom I have worked. Yet it was an acquaintance that had the most impression on me; I have never really "recovered" from it.

I was a teacher at Corentyne High when I first met Rudra. As senior master of Latin and English Literature, I was foolish enough to regard myself as important.

Rudra had just started Rose Hall High school at the former Rock Diamond Hotel. In those days all of us had a certain disdain for the unfortunates who could not get into Corentyne High and were forced to attend Rose Hall High. Some of this disdain we transferred to the principal. The big question was: what were the academic credentials of this principal. For in those days, academic credentials was everything. When we learnt, through the grapevine, that all he had was a GCE, we regarded him with some amusement. But when his school grew significantly in numbers, we began to think that maybe there was something more about this man. I was to discover that there was a lot more, more than what academic credentials can confer. In his presence I came to discover the power of spirituality. Rudra, by word and example, came to impress me so much that I still carry in my heart the deep lessons he implanted there.

The first was kindness. There was a deep compassion in him for every human being but especially for the poor and disabled. It shone in his demeanor and in his actions. I once saw him hug an epileptic boy in the fondest embrace. The inarticulate cries of joy that emanated from the mouth of the little boy, even as saliva drooled form his mouth onto to Rudra's clean white shirt, have never left my ears. Often Rudra would pick up in his car people on the road who were clearly exhausted from the hot sun and gave them a ride. I have seen him in earnest conversation with parents who could barely understand the words he was speaking but who were enthralled by the mere personality of the man: the earnestness in his face and the concern in his eyes were unmistakable. It was a sight to behold.

I left Corentyne High to teach with Rudra for a few months before I, too, left to start my own high school on the West Coast of Demerara. During those six months at Rose Hall High, two of which were in the new school on the reef, I grew to admire the sheer energy of the man, his passion for the noble work in which he was engaged, his remarkable vision for education on the Corentyne, his love for the common man. I even admired his verbosity: he took a long time to hammer home the points he was making but the sincerity of his message was evident throughout. I grew to love him. I accompanied him on our tour of the entire Corentyne, from Crabwood Creek to New Amsterdam in search of help for his new school. It was a long and difficult trek but we were all inspired by great leadership. There is absolutely no doubt that he inspired me as a principal of my own school. I learnt many things from him but I never acquired his gift for fund raising. I learnt, though, that daily admonitions to the entire school were a good thing. And so we had assemblies every day in which I preached the old virtues, quoted old poets, mainly Rabindranath Tagore, and reminded the students every day of the huge sacrifices their parents were making and appealing to them never to be ungrateful. I believe that these exhortations paid large dividends. I believe that many of my students grew up to be men and women who took care of their indigent parents. Quite a few immigrated to the United States and Canada and took their parents with them.

Rudra's influence has never left me even in my teaching careers in Canada. From him I learnt that if there was genuine concern for the students under my care, this could motivate them to achievement. From him I learnt affection for the "lowly and lost". My teaching career in Canda was immensely successful because I was fortunate to have encountered in my early career in Guyana a treasure, a deep spiritual and charismatic leader and friend who enabled me by his example to live a life of sacrifice, compassion and love. Whenever I think of Rudra I feel only gratitude, a sense of being uniquely blessed that Divinity chose me to be associated with such a remarkable man. Even as I sat as Chair of Federal Appellate Tribunal in the Judiciary of Canada, Rudra's compassion has never left my heart and his subtle presence was there in many of my decisions. Fortunately, the common law tradition of England allowed for such an attitude.

After I left the Corentyne, I heard that Rudra was involved in a costly lawsuit with his Board of Trustees in which he was accused of libel. He was found liable. I find this very ironic for a man who demonstrated so powerfully and so eloquently his concern for the public interest and for the common man. I was not a lawyer then. I wish I was. Then justice may have taken another course. At least the court would have heard the eloquence which Rudra inspired.

There are times when towards the end of his life a man reflects on the wonders he has encountered in his life. For me Rudra was certainly one of them. He was an icon.

VENUS NOEL (BANGAROO)

CLASS OF 1959

MY TRIBUTE TO THE LATE MR. RUDRA NATH

"FOUNDING FATHER OF ROSE HALL HIGHSCHOOL"

Mr. Nath was a visionary and caring individual. I recall when he came to Whim Village in 1959 and held a meeting which my father attended. He must have been very persuasive because the next thing I knew, I was enrolled in Rose Hall High School at "Rock Diamond" which, as we all know, was not an ideal location for a school. I was excited at the opportunity of going to high school when the future looked bleak for a choice of schools. It was also a relief for our parents, especially for girls, in planning for our future.

I would like to commend and thank Mr. Nath for his foresight in coming to the Corentyne to advocate for us "teenagers", to further our education, since the Opportunities for us were limited. He brought with him his team of teachers including Mr. Adarsh Hari, the youngest of the lot. A world of opportunities was ours to be explored and Mr. Nath and his teachers gave us a foundation under which to build and uplift our lives.

Mr. Nath ran a "tight ship"and it was his expectations and standards that we all had to adhere to, teachers as well as students. Mr. Nath had principles and was strict but compassionate. He was dealt a bad blow by the Board of Governors when we had to relocate and have a new school built. Much has been said about the building of the new school, which we all participated in, and where our education continued. The emphasis for the Class of January 1959 was for the preparation of the "College of Preceptors Exam" in December 1960. This was the stepping stone for all of us to realize our hopes, aspirations and future endeavors.

It is with great pride and joy that I was part of that experience, the Class of 1959. After leaving Rose Hall High School, following Senior Cambridge, I taught at Auchlyne Scot School and also attended Maggie Commercial School for shorthand and typing, and then wrote the English exam and got a distinction. I left for the U.K. in August 1965 and attended Kennington College in S.E. London and to my surprise Hardatt Punwasi was also a student. I left College and started my General Nursing training in September 1966 then my Midwifery and Neonatal Intensive Care Nursing at University College Hospital, London.

So with my Diplomas of S.R.N., S.C.M. and Neonatal training, I was ready to see the World and was about to undertake a two-year contract to Zambia but cancelled at the very end, as two years seemed a very long time then. When I received my Resident Visa for Canada with a job awaiting me in B.C in August 1975, while awaiting my application for a "Green Card" for the USA, I accepted and have never looked back. My training has served me very well. I retired in April 2012 and am still considered a valued member of my nursing team and community. I feel very fulfilled in my life. I have two grown children, both educated and independent young adults. They are my pride, two grandchildren and life goes on. My time will be spent on traveling, rest, relaxation and helping to raise the little ones.

Our Reunion, in Toronto in July 1995, honoring Mr. Nath was heartwarming and very emotional. The memories of our school years flooded my mind. It was wonderful to see Chumma, Vera, Chandra Ramkumar, Chandra Jag (the two of us taught at Auchlyne School), Chandrawattie Baichan, Oma, Bibi, Violet, Rubena, and others. As well as our male friends and the other 200 students.

I was fortunate to have visited with Mr. Nath in Fort Lauderdale over the years and shortly before his passing I was introduced to Mrs. Nath. I have always thought of Mr. Nath as our Principal and Educator. His later years were physically demanding and I would like to thank Mr. Hansram Ramrup for being a true friend, confidante and a caring individual, to Mr. Nath, to the very end. Hansram, you were helpful to him in so many ways and for that we are indebted to you.

We have all achieved so much in life, such as values, integrity, intelligence, wealth,

Knowledge, etc., which will be passed on to future generations. We shall not forget our humble beginnings, when compared to the North American Standard, yet we overcame living in various parts of the world and are valued members of society, at work, in our communities, our family and friends, all because of our background and education.

Knowledge is to be passed on and that is what Mr. Nath did. So, on behalf of my fellow students of the Class of 1959, it is with grateful hearts and thankfulness we applaud you for the successes we have all achieved.

Thank you, Mr. Nath. We Shall Not Forget.

TO OUR TEACHERS

A special "thank you!" to Mr. Adarsh Hari for his telling "the story" of Rose Hall High School and the other schools which my brother and three sisters attended.

It is with fond memories, classroom pranks and the dedication of our teachers:

Mr. Raymond Singh, (Math and Religious Knowledge); Mr. Haman Ben Yassim, (English Literature); Mr. Milton Latcha, (Latin); Mr. Vernon Asregadoo, (English and Geography); Mr. Julius Nathoo, (History); Mr. Hari, (Latin), Mr. Banerjee, (Hindi); Mr. Panday, (Math); Mr. Rawana, (Latin)and Mr. Yassin Sankar, (English Literature).

As teachers, you were so respectful of us and us likewise. We were at an impressionable age, 14 to 15 and onwards and all of you were approachable and very kind. Thank you all for embracing us and being a part of that journey in our young lives towards a secondary school education. You have helped to mold us into becoming the men and women we are today, proud and confident. Distance may separate us but the bond I share with a few of my classmates and closest friends will always be with me and I'm sure the same is to be said for many of us.

There were many incidents in my life that I credit to my family and educational background. I am forever grateful that I was born in Guyana where opportunities for girls were not limited to marriage but to education and where women were treated with respect and dignity.

You all did such a good job that when I was a nursing student my English patients would ask, "Nurse, where did you learn your English? (smile). My reply was, "My English was learned prior to coming to England."

Mr. Hari, you expressed that "Life is a wonderful gift." Indeed, it is! I know you like poetry so this poem is a favorite of mine:

"The clock of life is wound but once

And no man has the power

to tell just when the hands will stop

At late or early hour.

Now is the only time you own

Live, love, toil with a will

place no faith in time

for the clock may soon be still"

VERA DE GROOT PAUL

It is with humility and gratitude that I accept this invitation to share some of my memories of Rose Hall high School. Mr. Rudra Nath (deceased) in his infinite wisdom and knowledge was truly inspired to transform Rock Diamond Hotel into a place of learning, a school which benefited many of us and that paved the way for us to achieve success in the pursuit of happiness. Mr. Nath was compassionate, resolute and focused. He provided an opportunity for students to have a good education regardless of their nationality, religion or financial circumstances. He encouraged as to strive for excellence. He taught us to accentuate the positive, to be kind, honest, and respectful.

I started school in 1959. My first day was overwhelming. The building was old and inside decrepit. It was noisy and busy as the school was located in a business district, which was comprised of many stores. In spite of all these distractions, we, the students, bonded together. We were a very diverse group, but we were unique. The love we had for each other was inconceivable. The teachers were phenomenal.

Mr. Hari taught history. He was a good teacher dedicated, and caring. He was the epitome of gentleness. Mr. Hari you taught me humility. Mr. Yassim (deceased) taught literature. He was a good teacher also, very intelligent and intuitive. He understood our struggles as teenagers: peer pressure, disappointments and insecurities. He treated us with respect and dignity. Mr. Yassim, you taught me courage. Mr. Latcha taught Latin. He was a good teacher and a friend. He was Mr. Congeniality. Milton, you taught me spontaneity. Life is too precious to be nursing animosity and registering hate. Mr. Singh taught Math and Religious Knowledge. He was intelligent and dedicated. Geometry was a living nightmare for me. However, studying the synoptic Gospels (especially, St. Matthew), strengthened my faith. Mr. Singh you taught me forgiveness and unconditional love.

Mr. Vernon Asregadoo (relative) taught English and Geography. He was very intelligent, dedicated, compassionate and a role model. He was very cognizant of our complexity, diversity and temperament. He was non-judgmental and loving. Vernon was more than a teacher to us. He genuinely cared and wanted the best for us. He helpS us study for the GCE examination. English was a required subject. Vernon, you taught us well. You taught me moral values, accountability and responsibility.

To all the male teachers, Banerjee, Panday, Dhanraj, Nathoo. Peters, Rawana and Prashad (I.P) and the female teachers Prema, Bhajan and Shrinarine and my apology to any of those whose names I may have omitted inadvertently, I would like to take this opportunity to express my heartfelt gratitude to you. You have sacrificed your time to help us attain indomitable heights, but most of all, help us become better men and women. The world is a better place because of your contribution. I feel very blessed and honored to have been a student of RHS.

My fondest memory of Rose Hall High School, is working together in the 'swamp' at Rose Hall Village(waterside) helping to build our new school. It was tedious working in the heat of the sun. Sometimes, a few mosquitoes were let us feel their presence. As I sit here writing, my imagination brings to mind this beautiful picture of love and togetherness. A picture of us some pushing wheel barrows, some fetching blocks of concrete, some carrying water or performing other tasks. It was hard work but it was a labor of love. You my friends have left an indelible mark in my heart. We have formed lasting friendships. My thoughts and prayers will always with you.

CHANDRIDAT MADHO PERSAUD (PROFESSOR.)

ALUMINUS RHS

INDOMITABLE

Sankar's innocuous, scathing attack of the Tudors, Yasim's oratorical tirade on Tennyson, Gaj's simplified elucidation of Pythagoras, Prema's concern about the aberrant, illogical rules of grammar, Rawana's illumination of Caesar's Gallic campaigns and Rudra's hankering of platonic relationships, at Rose Hall High have imbued indelible memories that have forged my yin/yang, karmic/dharmic, existentialist essence.

The embryonic protests culminating in the RHS strike gave birth to my empowerment and from thence began a series of assaults against the 'establishment' - resignation from teaching at Mibicuri School in 1965, the first pink slip (and subsequent ones) resulting from the protests and strike against the Ministry of Education, the tussle with PNC hoodlums at UG, and my final resignation which resonated across the nation through Stabroek News" ENGLISH MASTER RESIGNS BECAUSE OF PRINCIPLE." I prospered as manager of Hand-In- Hand Insurance Company and diverted my resources to aiding humanity. The Lions School for the Blind in NA is testimony

The deep- rooted camaraderie at RHS stimulated the growth of relationships that would endure a lifetime. Our miniscule fraternity, ABC of RHS, started with the sons of three priests --Ajib, Bansrajh, and Chandridat. Two stalwarts, Somanlall and Jhagroo were soon inducted and, collectively we surmounted obstacles. In our sixties now, the fraternity has endured time, and time has been kind, for we have been married to our high school sweethearts, inculcated strong family values, and now look with pride to solidify our grandchildren's future.

Perhaps, Rudra's philanthropic ideals and the fraternal spirit of the ABC were responsible for the search of a cadre of humanitarians. My lionistic quest emanated at the Central Corentyne Lions Club. Then, I traversed the country and the Caribbean to help the sick, the needy, and the blind, moved to mentoring new clubs, established closer bond with Lionesses, and propelled CCLC into the limelight to become the premier club in Guyana and the Caribbean. As Zone Chairman, I was instrumental in the establishment of new clubs. As District Chairman for Guyana, Surinam, Trinidad and Tobago, I instilled the need to fight illegal drugs. And as I continue to provide support, present awards, make financial donations to organizations, I reminisce with pride my own International Award in Drugs and Alcohol Prevention.

RHS prepared me for the sardonic and vitriolic elements of the PNC who exercised vengeful discrimination and prejudice, and sledge hammered any semblance of my Indian identity. I introduced religious societies in many schools, and struggled to maintain my sanity against the tsunamic wave of political indoctrination and recrimination (transferred for being an undesirable in 1972). RHS provided a resurgence of the need to be vigilant. Armed with a deadly lance, I help to guard the school (RHS) against arsonists, during the period of racial unrest in 1963.That experience has culminated in my membership of the National Rifle Association of the US and a firm belief in the Second Amendment.

Young lads in colonial British Guiana faced a bleak future. Sankar would label it an educational limbo. Rawana would advise using Hannibal's strategies. Gaj's solution was always Pythagorean.... construct the house with a V roof and save the foundation. I had helped to build a V-roof school, and made friends with rattlesnakes, anacondas, and alligators in BBP. Then, the owls started hooting about a certain lagan's Night School. Cataclysmic but fortuitous!! Miss Prema had hinted at herculean tasks. Well, I guess tackling a couple of GCE Advanced Levels would be daunting but not insurmountable. I skipped English 100 at UG, completed the B.A. and the Dip. Ed., and wrote my first paper of 100 pages. Along the way I represented English and Humanities students at the Board of Trustees meetings. And now, at 66, the professor is energized, invigorated, and ready to turn the spade for another RHS. It all started with tectonic shifts in the sixties.

DWARKA PERSAUD

MY IMPRESSIONABLE DAYS AT

ROSE HALL HIGH SCHOOL

Reflecting back on the humble beginning of Rose Hall High School sometime in 1958, one cannot help but cherish the nostalgic feelings of those days, one cannot help but admire the pioneering spirit and iron will of its founder--Guruji, Rudra Nath, a true Brahmin in every sense of the word. It was his devine karma that propelled him to disseminate knowledge among the poor and down trodden.

Initially Rudra explored the possibility of establishing a secondary school at Bush lot on the West Coast of Berbice. This did not materialize and so he went to Rose Hall Village. Rudra hailed from West Coast Demerara. Exploring the idea of a high school as far as Berbice definitely entailed great courage and determination.

Rudra, the son of an indentured laborer (a driver at Uitvlugt) started from a humble beginning as a bicycle repair man. He gradually attained academic success at the GCE 'O' level. Subsequently, he started teaching at Guyana Oriental College. Having settled for Rose Hall Village as the site for his school he rented Rock Diamond hotel which was then a horse racing bookie. He brought along few teachers, Adarsh Hari, Odai Panday and Banergie.

I started school at the Rock Diamond Venue it was not the ideal environment- no playground, inadequate furniture, poorly ventilated rooms and in the center of rose Hall commercial district with noisy rum shops and restaurants nearby. Rudra and the students had a purpose and they stayed focus in their academic pursuit.

The school moved to the swamp area of Rose Hall in early 1961. Rudra solicited the help of local carpenters and builders who offered free services in order to build a one flat concrete structure. The early students--Birbahadur, Ramsaroop (deceased), Mangru, Punwasie, Dwarka, Permaul, Jagernath etc. worked at nights and the weekends to help cast concrete blocks. The one flat was quickly completed.

The school attracted students of poor families who could not afford or secure a place at the Queens College or at Corentyne High school--about a mile from Rose Hall High School. The students came from as far as Wellington Park on the East and Courtland #1 on the West. Children from poor family with extreme hardships were given free tuition scholarships.

The first set of students- 50 in all -took the first overseas exams. (The C.P) in 1960. The school had 43 passes- many with distinctions. The school again was ready for their Senior Cambridge exam. in1961. Of the Senior passes we had one grade 1; three grade 2 and several grade 3's. We were surprised to receive a congratulatory message from Mr. Chandi Singh of Corentyne high school for the fine performance of our school. I was fortunate to secure a grade 3 certificate. I then left Rose Hall in December, 1961 for home at Bush Lot on the West Coast of Berbice. I subsequently joined the Civil Service in 1962.

I personally benefited from the education offered at Rose Hall high school at the time. Were that not the case, I would have been condemned to the future in the rice fields or the cattle industry. I am extremely indebted to Guruji Nath and the school. I eventually pursue a successful Degree Programme and also a Post Graduate Studies at The University of Guyana in Geography and a Diploma in Education.The students from the Corentyne area greatly benefited from this school. The fees were low compared to other schools at the time. Rudra did not discriminate and I knew of a few Afro-Guyanese students who were given free tuition since their parents could not afford fees. They became nurses and teachers. Rudra should be immortalized.

ISHWAR PRASAD

Port Mourant /Corentyne Comprehensive High School... Sept.1961, Brttish Guiana not yet called Guyana, was coming of age and a greater awareness was growing on the people This was mostly due to the movement for independence from Britain led by Dr. Cheddi Jagan. It was 1960 and the world was changing very rapidly and people wanted to know more, to learn more. Port Mourant, the birthplace of Dr. Jagan was especially affected. The sugar factory, one of the largest and most successful, where many worked was closed down to punish the people for their fervent support of Dr. Jagan and his push for independence. The sugar workers were in the forefront, when pressure tactics, such as strikes, demonstrations and other forms of actions were called for and they persisted in their tactics even when threatened with loss of jobs and homes. People were also becoming more informed and interested in what was happening in the rest of the world and this was due to the fight for independence in other British and also French and Dutch colonies. Many of the young were leaving to study abroad also and more were eager to follow. We must not forget the contributions of our Test Cricketers, Rohan Kanhai, Basil Butcher, Joe Soloman, Ivan Madray (from Port Mourant), Lance and Glendon Gibbs, Roy Fredricks etc. who were followed on radio from England to India to Australia. The world and its affairs were becoming more and more familiar and the people wanted more.

Education was the key but there were limited options. There was need for more secondary/ high schools, as there was only one in the area, Corentyne High, but three primary schools graduating hundreds of students who could not find places and so were forced to give up on their education. In 1958, Mr.Rudra Nath had started Rose Hall High but that was not enough, as students were coming from other parts of Corentyne as far away as Skeldon to try and further their education.

So, it was that Mr. John Muria, a long-time teacher at St. Francis Xavier Catholic, got together with Mr. David Matlay and Mr. Samuel Asregadoo of St. Joseph Anglican, to start a new high school. Mr. Muria was the most involved. He was slated to be the Principal of the new school and so he proceeded to look for a suitable building and to recruit students. A building from the closed Port Mourant factory was selected but it would cost $4000.00 to buy it. This was a formidable sum, but it was obtained when forty people gave $100.00 each. In Sept.1961 Port Mourant Comprehensive Institute was opened, with Mr. Muria as principal and James Permaul, Paul Kewalall, Walter Balmakund, and Elaine Mallay as teachers. Miss Mallay would also be the school secretary.

The idea was to create a school that taught, not only the traditional subjects but also practical ones like Typing (this was mainly to appeal to parents to send their daughters, whose education was sadly lacking). There was a trickling of students at first. Mr Muria, his teachers and some members of the community went out on recruiting trips all over the neighboring areas to inform parents of the new school and also to collect funds to help in the running of the school. It was a slow and difficult task but eventually will become a roaring success. Unfortunately, even though a fee was charged and some money was collected, it proved to be too little to pay teachers' salary and other expenses. Mr. Muria who had a large family could not afford to remain as principal and he returned to his position at St. Francis Xavier and, I was recruited to replace him. I had been teaching at Berbice High School (one of the elite schools founded by the Presbyterians), but my father (who was one of the 40), persuaded me to accept the position. I was very skeptical, was 19 years old, had a very good salary and had been teaching for only two years. Looking back, it was one of the best decisions that was made for me as the next seven years would prove to be very challenging but some of the best years of my life, both teaching and otherwise. This is where l honed my teaching and management skills. Here is where I made life-long friends. Here is where I met some remarkable young men and women, who would go on to great successes, at home and abroad. Here is where I grew, together with the teachers (i) and the students.

The next couple of years were difficult. The building was not suitable. We were constantly buffeted with noise, sand and heat. It was remarkable to see the students laboring under these trying conditions, but labored they did and quite successfully. We had almost immediate good results, first at the College of Preceptors and then at the GCE examinations. I had introduced two new subjects that were not taught at the other high schools, Economics and British Constitution (James Smith had already introduced Biology) and the students took well to them, as well as the traditional courses of English, Math, Geography etc. We continued to teach Typing but students wanted more, so after a while we dropped it. In sports we excelled with our cricket, and table tennis teams.

In the meantime, the other, more established Rose Hall High was having problems, not academic, as they were doing quite well, but management.

They were forced to move from their building to the Port Mourant race course. This was an awful place for teaming and so talks were held with us for a merger, as we had the space. The talks were successful and the merger took place in early, 1964. Under the terms of the merger, Mr. Rudra Nath would remain as Principal, until the completion of the school year. I was to be Senior Vice-principal and would take over as Acting Principal when Mr. Nath left and Mr. Vernon Asregado would be Vice-principal. The school was to be renamed Corentyne Comprehensive High School and would have an enrollment of almost one thousand and a new building would be made.

There were some tension between the two staffs and between the two student groups. We had been competitors academically and on the sports field but gradually things began to improve and soon we were on our way. Mr. Nath was very involved and very successful in raising funds and I was left to run the school, when he was away. We were able to expand the library and the students settled down. They were an eclectic group, coming from miles around and they were eager to learn in this much more accommodating, comfortable place.

Mr. Nath, who had done yeoman service over the years, and laid the foundation for what would be the new school, left to start another school, National High (as there continued to be demand for secondary education). Vemon Asregado had already left to start a new school in the Novar/ Mahaicony area and I, together with the thirty or so teachers, were left to build on what they had started.

In 1966, Mr. Walter Ramdehol, was hired as Principal and I was to be Vice-principal. Mr. Ramdehol had years of experience as a teacher and Administrator and during his tenure (viii) continued to uphold the high standards that had been built at the school. Academically, the students flourished and in sports we reached new Heights with our cricket, volleyball and table tennis. I left Comprehensive in 1968 to further pursue my studies in Montreal and then in Hamilton, Canada. In Jan. 1972, I was hired by Sir George Williams University to teach Political Science. Over the next thirty-five years, wherever I have taught and whatever success I have had (no matter, the title I was hired under, I was always a teacher first and foremost). This was due mainly to my experiences at Comprehensive.Those challenging / trying / learning conditions have been truly worthwhile.

(1) NAMES OF THE TEACHERS WHO TAUGHT AT PORT MOURANT COMPREHENSIVE INSTITUTE & CORENTYNE COMPREHENSIVE HIGH SCHOOL...

Asregadoo Vernon (Ass. Principal), Bacchus Azim, Birbahadur Mohanlall, Boodram Dennis, Etwaroo leslie, Hari Adarsh, Haripersaud 'Brazo', Joseph Ralph, Kewalall Lakraj, Lall Soman, Madray Somdat, Nagamootoo Moses, Naidoo Kenneth, Narine Chandradutt, Nath Rudra, (Principal), Permaul James, Persaud Kesso, Peters Samuel, Prashad Ishwar (Ass. Principal/ Principal), Prema Hanna, Punwassie Hardutt, Sanichar Sagar, Walter Ramdehol, (Principal), Ramkeerat Subas, Ramkissoon Chunilall, Ramnarine Gajraj, Rawana William, Roopan Mahendranath, Shrinarine Doromattie, Singh Julip, Sukra Prema, Surujpaul Jatischand, Yassim Haman Ben.

HARRI RAMCHARRAN

The founding of Rose Hall High School in 1958 was a boon for many parents desiring their children to attend high school. Corentyne High School (Chandi), the only reputable one in central Corentyne, could not accommodate the excess demand. I started in 1959 at RHS and was happy to be with friends from the Bush-Lot-Alness area and from Albion C.M. Despite the crowded classrooms and inadequate physical facilities, the students had a deep desire to be educated and to excel. The teachers did not fail to meet the students' expectations; their dedication and commitment to teaching was par-excellence, so was their patience with students who needed additional help. First impression is always indelible. In Form I, I was deeply impressed/motivated by Mr. Hari who taught Latin, Geography, History, and Literature, and by Mr. Panday the three branches of Mathematics (Arithmetic, Algebra, and Geometry). Besides the subject matter, I learnt from them the craft/skill of effective teaching which I ended up doing as a career. I spent one term in Form I and another in Form II, then couple of us were promoted to Form III to prepare for the CP exam within a two yearS span rather than the three. It was challenging but we were in the hands of competent and dedicated teachers, Mr. Asregadoo, Mr. Latcha, Mr. Raymomd Singh, and Mr. H.B. Yassim. Some classes were challenging. Mr. Latcha, with infinite patience and passion, explained the use of the subjunctive mood in Latin. Mr. Yassim, with consummate flair, emphasized the importance of understanding figures of speech in order to appreciate poetry /literature; the "onomatopoeia" and the "alliteration" in the poem "Lepanto" were his prime examples, but his best was "classical allusion "when pertained to Bacchus, the Roman god of wine /revelry. One teacher, Mr. Banerjee, was very liked for other reasons; he was shy and never made eye contacts with the class; at times it appears like he was talking to himself muttering unintelligible words. Banar (as Parasar called him) always pronounced the name PUCK (the character in Shakespeare's Midsummer Night's Dream) as PAAK; everything appeared comedic/hilarious and we found it difficult to restrain our laughter. Learning was enjoyable; the sparkling personalities of Parasar, Arjunen and Khuba made the atmosphere in class stimulating, relaxing and humorous. The results of the CP exam were very good; many students earned distinctions in many courses; the teachers and the community were proud of the newly established school.

Preparation for Senior Cambridge was a smooth transition, but with higher level of motivation and enthusiasm because a "credit" at the SC level was equivalent to a "pass" at the GCE "O" level. A new teacher, Mr. J. Nathoo, made significant improvemnt to the quality of the program; he taught Latin and History. His tests were rigorous; parts of the Latin tests were from past GCE exams; also rumor had it that his history lectures were good enough to pass the "A" level. His Socratic method (the teacher-student dialogue interaction) of teaching was interesting, he relished intellectual challenges. The results of the Cambridge exam were very good; RHS was recognized as a premier secondary school. It was great learning experience at

RHS; Mr. Nath encouraged a lot of creative activities; debate, singing, poetry writing, impromptu speech etc. There was a group of multi-talented students; Ivan Harry (Bug) singing "the banana boat" song, and "Till the end of time"; Rahim Baksh reciting Tagore's poem, Premchand Das singing songs from the Indian movie, "Paying Guest", also Eileen Bhajan was the poet laureate.

It was during this time the spirit of self-help was inculcated through fund raising activities by students and teachers to renovate the RHS building and later to build the new school at the "reef" as enrollment increased.

At RHS, we were teenagers, we were restless searching for our individual identity, looking for heroes/heroines, and trying to establish a positive self-esteem through academic excellence. RHS provided us with this avenue for this self- discovery through the astute leadership of Mr. Nath. We also did lots of the "regular" things, pranks, teasing, harmless flirting (an intellectual stimulant), etc. There were few cases of students being suspended from class for minor infractions. The best of all, however, love was always in the air; a lot of crushes, secret love, unrequited love, and broken hearts. Many students also met their future spouses at RHS. One uncomfortable situation for me was when Mr. Nathoo appointed me as prefect – extraordinaire (whatever it means); to my amazement the responsibility was to report the students who smoked during break at Hilton and Coppin's parlors. Thank God, like the proverbial monkey, I see nothing, hear nothing, and say nothing. Ironically, once in a while I used to give my "small change" to one of the regulars to buy cigarettes. He also gave me the nickname "the smiling brunette", I guess because of my somber outlook.

After graduating with Senior Cambridge, I joined the civil service (Ministry of Health). Traveling to New Amsterdam (25 miles each way) was hectic so I quitted after a year and joined Kildonan Scots School as a teacher. In 1968 one of my best friends, Stanley Permaul (an outstanding student at RHS) was planning to attend college in the USA; he urged me to join him after he established himself abroad, I did so in 1969. To be brief, I graduated with a PhD degree in International Economics from State University of New York-Binghamton in 1977. I taught at State University of New York College at Cortland for five years, and then joined the University of the West Indies/Jamaica in the Institute of Economic Research for three years. Since 1986 I have been at University of Akron (OHIO) as Professor of Finance and International Business. I have established a fruitful and enjoyable career whose foundation was at RHS. A proud event in my professional life was an invitation in 2006 to participate at The Oxford University Round Table Conference on International Trade and the Environment. From RHS to Oxford is a great and a unique achievement; many other students (and teachers) from RHS have also distinguished themselves in other disciplines/professions. I love to communicate about events at RHS with other students, especially the iconic Chunmattie Gurbatoor whose memory and in-depth knowledge of people and events qualify her for an honorary PhD. I would like to dedicate the following verses to:

(A) THE TEACHERS OF RHS. FROM "THE BEST SCHOOL OF ALL" BY HENRY NEWBOLT

"The men that tanned the hide of us,
Our daily foes and friends,
They shall not lose their pride of us,
Howe'er the journey ends
Their love, to us who sing of it,
No more its message bears,

But the round world shall ring of it
And all we are be theirs."

(B)TO OUR DEAR PRINCIPAL MR. NATH (MAY HE REST IN PEACE). FROM "THE VILLAGE SCHOOLMASTER" BY OLIVER GOLDSMITH

"The village master taught his little school;
A man severe he was, and stern to view;
I knew him well, and every truant knew;
Well had the boding tremblers learn'd to trace
The day's disasters in his morning face,
Full well they laughed with counterfeited glee,
At all his jokes, for many a joke had he:
Full well the busy whisper, circling round,
Convey'd the dismal tidings when he frown'd:
Yet he was kind; or if severe in aught,
The love he bore to learning was in fault.
The village all declared how much he knew."

(c) To RHS. From "The best school of all" by Henry Newbolt

"We'll honor yet the school we knew,
The best school of all,
We'll honor yet the rule we knew,
Till the last bell call.
For, working days or holidays,
And glad or melancholy days,
They were great days and jolly days
At the best school of all."

MOHAMED FREZLUDEEN RAUFMAN
(1962-1964)

I am Mohamed Frezludeen Raufman. I attended Rose Hall High School for 2 ½ years. Before writing the GCE exam, I had to leave school. My reason was financial. I could not afford to continue. After migrating to Canada, I continued high school and finished with a grade 12 in Toronto. I then went on to trade school

What I want to be clear is that if it were not for Mr. Rudra Nath and Rose Hall High School I do believe that I will not know what a high school education is all about. Rose Hall High School gave me the opportunity to have a high school education and make me realize how important education is. This gave me a insight to want to achieve a higher education.

After finishing primary school at 16, there was no hope for me towards a higher education unitl Mr. Nath, the Principal of Rose Hall High School gave me that opportunity to attend school. I will forever be grateful to Mr. Nath and Rose Hall High School teachers. It was this school that opened doors for me and for a thousand other students.

SAGAR SANICHAR

REMEMBERING THE STRUGGLES

Sagar Sanichar was a teacher with RHS and CCHS throughout their educational journey. The impact of education is emphasized.

In the fall of 1959 Mr. Rudra Nath made his bold effort to provide secondary education in the lower Corentyne area. It was an honor and pleasure to be under the gentle but professional guidance and leadership of principals Rudra Nath, John Muria, Walter Ramdehol and their deputies,Vernon Asregadoo and lshwar Prashad. These gentlemen imbued and impressed us all to recognize the dignity of teaching. »Primus inter Pares » (First among equals) was the philosophy of Walter Ramdehol. The teachers responded respectfully and did their best for the students. There were friendly and genuine professional relationships among teachers and between teachers and students-- real educational fun.

Despite the lack of fewer educational facilities and ideal conditions the students did brilliantly.- both in academics and sports. Voluntary Saturday and evening classes helped. Quite a number of students went on to excel and then distinguish themselves in various areas of education and professions. Lawyers, teachers, politicians, professors, technicians, corporate owners and executives, brokers and so on, are trademarks of these schools. To emphasize, among former students, BA's, MA's, RN's, CPA's. PhD's, etc are not surprises.

Prior to 1959 limited high schools space and affordability prevented a large number of primary school leaving students from attending high schools. Few were fortunate to be office or factory workers in the sugar industry. Others helped in their parents' farms; few enrolled in private trade outfits. A small number of girls opted for typing schools while a larger number assisted at home, learning to be seamstresses and waiting to be matrimonially matched. Sewing machine retailers had bumper years during this period. A good number of boys, providing financial assistance at home, were sucked into the sugar industry doing slavish jobs under the most disagreeable conditions.

Rose Hall High School and Corentyne Comprehensive High School saw increased enrollment, especially for girls. Most of these students were from poor families who sacrificed their meager incomes for their children's high school education. High school education was not free but these poor families did their best. It was their pride, joy and dignity to see their children attend high schools. This scenery changed beautifully: a very large number of neatly uniformed students hurrying to their respective high schools were a delightful site.

Education is absolutely necessary to help change the world for the better. We can, for example, admire the thoughts of Gandhi, Sir Thomas Moore and Mark Twain and reject Nietzsche. We should all improve conditions that can make education more comfortable and enjoyable.

Refections of Rose Hall High School

By Chandra Jagnandan Seecharran

To think of my years at RHS, is like going back in time....another life time ago, the years that set my future in motion.

Rose Hall High School was a place of real hard work and dedication, comradeship, unity and belonging. We felt love and friendship towards all our classmates, and have formed lasting bonds We were like one big happy family, This was all due to the caring and personable attitude of our beloved principal, Mr Rudra Nath. It was because of this reason that I refused to switch over to Corentyne High School, when a teacher was sent to recruit me. I felt quite settled with my new family at Rock Diamond and insisted on staying there in spite of the protest from my family.

Apart from the academic training, we did fund-raising for the new school, and had a lot of hands on experience. My cousin, Rohini Jagpat and I had several opportunities to attend yagnas, satsangs and concerts in the company of Mr Nath, Miss Prema and his nephew to raise money for the new school. We did well and had a great time doing it.

I am fondly remembering many of the teachers. They were all friendly courteous and unintimidating. I cannot forget during the first term in one of Mr Hari's classes. He was so wrapped up in getting his point across that he said very seriously, giving an analogy "like a man jukking a post". Suddenly, the whole class was dying of laughter. He politely asked what was so funny. He was then asked if there was such an English word as "juk". He became embarrassed, but soon joined in the laughter. He was a good sport. Lots of respect to Mr. Nath, Vernon Asregado, Miss Prema, Teacher Hari, Mr. Nathoo and all the other teachers who made school what it was.

Needless to say, this is where many of us met our future spouses or first love. Romance was always in the air, in spite of the strict watchful eyes of the principal. Who can stop nature from taking its course.

Sad to say, many of our beloved ones like Mr Nath, Rohini, Lainmattie,Rebecca Kanhai,Chandrawattie Bachan, Zainool, Sheikh and many others have passed on.There is a special place in my heart for them. May God bless their souls!.

My Reflections of Rose Hall High School

By Jai Seecharan

I was only 17, still wet behind the ears, and finished high school nearly a year ago. I was too young to get employed anywhere, except in my father's shop. He knew that I did not enjoy being in the shop and did not want me to get used to being a" loungera" He spoke to Mr. Nath about me teaching at the school. The school did not have money to employ another teacher, so it was decided that I would be a volunteer with no pay. Somehow, I started getting paid after my second month, February 1961.

I remember those eight months as amongst the best times of my life. It was a great learning Experience for me. I learnt so much from the Principal about life. He showed the teachers and the students how to live. His discipline was administered with great love, and that is the reason many of his students loved, rather than feared him. He made everyone of us feel that we were important, and we should be proud of what we were. What a contrast to my alma mater! I still remember I once attended the Tirth (Teerat) at the beach.The next day, a large number of students were not allowed to enter class because we missed class. We received a strong lecture, making us feel guilty of participating in our religious activities. That and the attitude of some of the other teachers made me feel uncomfortable being a Hindu. We were still at Rock Diamond during Phagwah, and as I passed through a doorway, there was Wattie, my friend, waiting for me. I felt like a little mouse in the clutches of a big cat. She must have emptied a whole can of powder on me. The Principal, teachers and students forgot who they were and played Phagwah the way it was meant to be.

I enjoyed the trips Mr Nath, Miss Bhajan, Miss Prema and other teachers would take to visit parents. Sometimes we would go to recruit students, other times we would go because of a serious illness or death in the family... Many of these students would not have attended high school had it not been for the encouragement of Mr Nath. A few of them were already sixteen or seventeen years old. I remember one of them used to terrorize me, maybe because he did not want to be in school or because he was older than me.

While the new school was being built, students and teachers would take turns being"watchman". Milton Latcha, myself and a couple senior students decided to make a bucket of cook up rice, (we did not have a pot) since we had a fire to scare away the thieves, ghosts and mosquitoes .

Who could forget the young talent that was exposed during the concerts and songs like "Dil Apna aur Preet Paraye" by Shanti and songs by heartthrob Raymond Singh. School was indeed fun for the teachers as well as for the students. Feisty students like Rohinee, Chunmattie, Sheila, Bibi, Uma, Mendonsa, Jhoot, Mahendra and a long list of others cannot be separated from the memories of RHS. Students were shown how to remove the boundaries, set by themselves or others. I have always said that the students and teachers made the greatest advancement because they had to struggle against the greatest odds. Many of them now rank as great as anyone else who had started out at the prestigious high schools in Guyana. Hardatt Poonwasie is a good example of an international known architect.

During my emotional farewell speech, I said that even though I was leaving, my heart will remain at RHS. Not too many caught on that I was leaving it with someone special. Was the joke on my dad? Did he realize that he let the mongoose in the fowl pen, or did he do it intentionally ?

ISAAC (ABO) SURINARAIN

I, Isaac Surinarain, known as a Abo, was born at Port Mourant, Berbice, Guyana, South America. I now live in New York since 1992. I am married to a wonderful wife who is still my support and inspiration and the blessed mother of my eight children – five boys and three girls. I am blessed with four grandchildren. I am exceedingly proud of my children being who they are. Having come to this country and after being certified as a fire safety director in the operation , maintenance and record keeping from the Fire Department of the City of New York and realizing the worth of education, I and my wife encouraged my children to get a good education – the passport to success. Today, the majority of my children do have Bachelor's degrees, holding great jobs, and are doing exceptionally well while living good lives.

When I met Mr. Rudra Nath he was very impressed with my history in both Table Tennis and in Cricket. He wanted me in his school as a coach to guide the children in these two areas. As he hoped to make his school #1 in education and this includes the sports. A little reflection in the areas of my expertise (Table Tennis and Cricket) will indicate that in his eyes he saw my qualifications to work for him and that I would be only too honored to work in the service of his school.

My history in table tennis spans 23 years from 1956 to 1978. I won several table tennis championships. I was the individual table tennis champion at the Port Mourant community Center for over 10 years; the Berbice individual table tennis champion against the dynamic Latchman Doobay-- a match that was gruelling, intense and very competitive-- and this title I held for 10 years. Then I won the Guyana Sugar Estates individual championship. This title I held for one year. I became the first Senior Table Tennis Player to reach semi-final in Guyana Individual Table Tennis Championship from Berbice. When in Surinam Berbice played Surinam in the team and individual championships, we were successful there also. In this match I won the individual championship. And when Berbice played Georgetown, with Latchman Doobay and I representing Berbice against two national players, Monte Clark and M. Draton, I won the first round, beating Monte and Draton, but lost to Godfrey Denny (a national player) in a 2 sets to 3 in the semi final. Here the eyes of the nation watched and discovered that Berbice has superb and outstanding players. As a player I must say that I have been greatly honored to play against Richard Bergman, from England who won seven world championship during his professional career.

I have been playing inter-county cricket from 1961 to 1976 – a period about 15 years. I also played cricket and table tennis for Guyana.

In the field of cricket, I have made 27 single hundred runs including many lower scores in the 60s and 70s. The following statistics are good measuring rods that capture some of the highlights in my cricket career.

In the first big cricket match at Port Mourant Community Center in the Davson Cup Cricket Competition, (regarded as First Class Cricket Competition in Berbice only), I took a hattrick in the first inning and in the second inning with four deliveries I took three wickets (a record that's still outstanding). In the same Davson match competition, I became the first batsman to make three (one hundred runs) successively in three different matches.

In the Campbell Cup Sugar Estates Cricket Competition (where first class cricket was played for all the Sugar Estates in Guyana), I played for the Berbice Cricket Team from 1961-1976 (15 years). In the final cricket match played at the Port Mourant Community Center Grounds between the Berbice Sugar Estates Cricket Team and the Demerara Sugar Estates Cricket Team, I made an outstanding one hundred and seven runs. This was the first hundred runs made in a first class cricket match since the opening of the Port Mourant Community Center Grounds. In honor of this great feat I was awarded a prize bat from the Port Mourant Community Center Sports Council. I have made outstanding scores in other cricket endeavors. When Berbice played Essequibo at the Georgetown Grounds, I made one hundred and eighty six runs and when Berbice played Surinam in Surinam my top score was over one hundred runs.

In the Kewall Cup Competition, in the match played in Trinidad by the Guyana Indian cricket Team against the Trinidad Indian Cricket Team, I made three hundred and six runs in six innings. I was presented a bat by the Trinidad Cricket Board as the best batsman during the series. I also played against, Australia, England, Jamaica, Pakistan and St. Kitts. Yes, I am happy to play against so many countries.

In the areas of table tennis and cricket I have been able to represent, with greatest satisfaction and a deep sense of endearing pride, my beloved Berbice and my dear country, Guyana. I am proud to say that I have been named Berbice Sportsman of the Year –for one year ; and was highlighted in the Awards Sports Section in the

Guyana Newspaper. To my native Berbice and my beloved country, I am deeply indebted to you both and am glad to have served as a native son.

Although my successes and accomplishments are largely due to my initiative, dedication and hard work, I would like to express my gratitude to Basil Butcher, my neighbor from whom I learned the essentials of cricket. Besides, he was very kind and helpful and very supportive always making sure I was not short for any cricket gears. Then there was Eric Nankoo. He was Port Mourant Community Center caretaker, youth club leader and table tennis coach. He would often keep the facility open and even gave us refreshments. Then there was Joe Soloman who coached us to play the game of cricket in the correct way. He was Guyana's best cricket coach, in my opinion.

Mr. Nath hired me officially as a table tennis and cricket coach .At that time we were at Rahaman Race Course Pavillion. Later, we moved to Corentyne Comprehensive High School. I also was to help Mr. Austin (part-time) in the Cafeteria. I stayed there for nine years Mr. Nath asked me to work with Chando Narine, the games master. I was able to coach in the areas of table tennis and cricket. Soon our school was highlighted not only as number one for academics but also number one for sports – volleyball, table tennis and cricket.

The following students have brought great honors to our school in their outstanding achievment; some in the field of cricket; others in table tennis and some in both fields.

Honorable mention must be given to Alvin Kallicharran who made tremendous impact in bringing cricket to the limelight. It seems that Alvin was born to play cricket. At one time, he was the best left-handed batsman in the world. Alvin was at one time the captain for Guyana and also for the West Indies Cricket Teams. In the game of cricket, Alvin brought to Guyana international fame and acclaim for his unique and excellent marksmanship and sportsmanship.

Then, there is Anand Sookram. He was outstanding in both table tennis and cricket. He won championships in both the junior as well as the senior divisions. Anand was the junior table tennis champion for Berbice, Guyana and the Caribbean, and the Senior table tennis Champion for Berbice and the Guyana Sugar Estates. He won the table tennis championship from me after I kept the title for ten years. In the field of cricket Anand was superb. He was excellent as a left arm spin bowler and was a superb batsman.

Other outstanding players of honorable mention at CCHS who highlighted table tennis as well as cricket and volleyball and who not only brought great honors to our school but who went on to achieve national fame: M. Madramootoo, S. Kallicharran, K. Singh,… (National cricketers).

Those who deserve special mention at CCHS: G.Appanah, K. Budram, B. Puran, R. Arjune,… (Outstanding in Cricket and Table Tennis) L. Ganesh. C. Baldeo, A.Khan, H. Ketwaru and H. Permaul… (Outstanding in Cricket). Also, all the other players who participated and added to the glory of CCHS, I would like to mention that we owe you a special thank you for all you have given us.

I would like to remember Mr.Nath,– a little man with a big heart; a man with a dream and a vision and a man who was very versatile. It was he who emphasized and made it happen that education should be extended to all – both boys and girls. Mr.Nath also encouraged me to pursue my education which I did and for which I am most grateful.

Then there was Iswar Prashad. Special thanks for his insight, encouragement, and cooperation and his helping hand to foster sports at CCHS. Also special thanks be extended to Walter Ramdehol for his genuine support and contributions in the area of sports.

Also, great thanks to James Austin, the caretaker and my friend with whom I worked in the cafeteria. He was indispensable as a worker and was a genuine supporter-- a man with a heart of gold.

Finally, I like to thank my dear friend, Adarsh Hari for being a real true friend and for encouraging me to write my history. I am so glad to be given this great opportunity. Adarsh ... Glad you are doing this!!!

HUGH TODD
AKA
HUGH WILLIAMS

I was standing at Hilton's shop, gaffing with some friends and soaking up the refreshing breeze in the cool afternoon. Most of my friends were older than I. But my mind was not on the conversation. Across the street, parents were taking their children to be enrolled in the new high school which was to be opened shortly at the Rock Diamond Hotel building. My mind was in a turmoil. How can I be enrolled too? I have to make a life- changing decision. And it had to be now! My friends noticed my uneasiness and wondered what was my problem. Without hesitation, I release myself from my companions into the street and appeared in the waiting line. Apparently, I was the only one without a parent, but Mr.Nath accepted me.

When classes commenced in April 1959, there were about 40 students in Form 3 but the numbers swelled to about sixty. Within 15 to 17 months we were scheduled to write the College of Preceptors Examination (C P). We all persevered. In the evenings, a group of us, namely, James Woode, Clifford Mann, Ivan Harry, Lawrence

Chapman, Arjunen Permaul, John Mangra and Hardat Punwassie, burned the books into the early mornings then reported for school a few hours after.

We took up the challenge to work towards this goal. There was so much information to understand and retain; and concepts to grasp. World geography was one of my pet disciplines. Studying maps and finding ways to remember facts brought quite a lot of humor. For instance, we used our own imagery. Italy is shaped like a boot. Cecily is near the sea. So, Italy kicks Cicely to the sea. It was a tall order. But with commitment and determination we succeeded. The dividends paid off. Each of us passed with one or more distinctions. It was a crowning achievement. God rewarded us for our tireless effort.

To attend Rose Hall High School was an unimpeachable decision I did make in my youth. It was the catalyst that steered my life to manhood and concretized my modest accomplishments. My contemporaries continued their education at the school and passed the Senior Cambridge examinations while I moved on to short stints of teaching at Port Mourant Catholic School and Farley High School in my village. At the latter school, I taught students for the College of Preceptors Examination and they performed very well. While teaching, I studied privately for the General Certificate of Examination (GCE) and was successful.

The desire to broaden my horizon; to see the world outside of my little village, made me journey to the capital, Georgetown, in 1965. The General Post Office was my first stop. A few months later, upon learning about a vacancy for a teacher at Campbell's Academy at Eccles, I reported there and was promptly hired by one, Mrs. Iris Vierra. I prepared students for CP, and the General Certificate of Examination, and garnered many passes in both. My stint there was rewarding and fulfilling but I just could not control the restlessness inside.

The escapism bug stung my feet. In 1968 I journeyed 69 miles to the bauxite town, by ferry, to the then Mackenzie. A few years ago, I was in Berbice, then Georgetown, now I was at another extreme. But why? However, I was fortunate to meet a villager whose brother was head of a private high school. So, without hesitation I was soon employed. Literature was one of the disciplines I really enjoyed teaching. Getting students to immerse themselves in the action and meaning of the story helped them to fully understand and realize the impact of the interplay of emotions that make poetry come alive. A few of my students were moved to tears as we studied the poems, "Sohrab and Rustum" by Matthew Arnold and "Michael" by William Wordsworth. I must pause here to let you know that it was because of my literature teacher, Mr. Yassin Sankar, at Rose Hall High School that made me gravitated to literature and to love poetry. Thus, while at school I began writing poems.

Over the years, I have written numerous poems which have not been published. Some are published in two collections of my own: "The Poet's Song" and "Window of my Mind". I have contributed to the anthologies, Dance on the Horizon, The Eternal Sea, The Best Poems of 2005, and Theatre of my Mind published by the International Library of Poetry; also to the anthologies, Treasury of Guyanese poetry; Ten Anniversary (1966-1976) Guyanese Writings compiled and edited by A. J. Seymour.

Later in January 1971, I taught at the Wismar Hill School in the secondary department. And as usual I prepared students for CP and, inter-school debating competitions. Wismar High School became one of the top debating schools during my tenure there. This school will always have lasting memories for me, not only as a trained teacher, but as a bachelor, renouncing his singleness to unite with my wife,

Esther and becoming a father of two children.

After nine years, I ventured out again. The bauxite company became my last and final sojourn. I started at the communications department and ascended the promotion ladder. Between 1983 to 1996, I held the position of editor of the Communications Department, Senior Management Training Officer, Principal of the Technical Training Complex and Manager of the Linden Television Station. During my tenure there, I acquired a wealth of knowledge, information and skills and develop the attitude that truly broadens my horizon; thereby, enhancing perspective of the world around me.

REFLECTIONS

Reflections are usually a blend of the good and the undesirable events in our lives, the successes and failures. But they always etch out lasting memories which would eventually shape or charter the courses of our lives to be the persons we would be in the future. We who were the first batch of Rose Hall High School, relish being the trail blazers. We did our duty to the expert teaching of young men who today would be considered untrained teachers. But to us they were the best! We admired their perseverance and resilience under the grand leadership of the principal, Mr. Rudra Nath. I do conjecture on what lured Mr. Nath to leave the Essequibo Region to sojourn to Rose Hall Village to open a High School. Maybe, it was divine intervention. He knew not whether his dreams would be fulfilled. He took the chance and succeeded against the odds. Many parents were very low income workers or self- employed. Many of us, youths, of Rose Hall were rescued from the cul-de-sac of a high school education. Many of us of that batch had already passed the Primary School Leaving Examination and were wondering what next. The opportunity to proceed to Corentyne High School was not possible because our parents did not have the means to support us. Also we were above the age to be trained as pupil teachers. Mr. Nath gave us that privilege to achieve our dreams since his fees were lower. What a social transformation for young villagers! After my first day at school, my friends whom I often met at Hilton's shop were excited about my progress, that they immediately pinned the name "schoolboy" on me. It became my household name even unto today. The achievement of Rose Hall High School was of no mean success. The multiplying effect produced teachers, law enforcement officers, engineers among others. Today, as I redirect my thoughts to 1959, I am humbled and yet proud that I patiently waited in the line and with others created an historical moment in time.

A Commentary: "Againist All Odds"

By Dennis Boodram*

"Against All Odds" is a "collective wonderment", whereby Adarsh Hari gives us a dignified collaboration of experiences and thoughts and a safe journey back in time. Through the contributors, he portrays to the discerning reader the legacy of an institution, a noble one I must mention, to future generations. I enjoy reading the many stories, spotlighted on personal experience. The compilation is carefully presented, albeit without offense.

After reading the essays, I realize that we have transcended our past and that everyone has a story to tell. The strength of "Against All Odds" lies in the adamant insistence that each person or group reflects on the prevailing contemporary culture and focuses on providing "the utmost" to a wanting society.

The teachers and students who contributed help one to understand that they were certain in their uncertainty. Uncertain in their next step forward but devoted to the pursuit of a higher education and that's the certainty. Adarsh himself makes the point that the growth and development of the schools were rooted in events. These events caused the people of the prevailing society – the Berbecians – to be extracted out of their sentimentality and to be taken up in the realm towards "the pursuit of a higher education".

"Against All Odds" came out of conviction and convergence of those who battled against "the odds". There were those who might not have shared in the journey and will become a flippant and unfamiliar. That is why Adarsh let each contributor share his/her personal journey – one of hope, vision and dreams.

I detect identity by each contributor in heart and spirit. Adarsh supposedly could have interviewed each contributor and compiled it in his own research and present us with his works. Instead, he unselfishly extracted from a cross - section of former students and teachers and let them tell their story.

In my personal association with Adarsh, I know that his belief in education is fundamental as opposed to just believing in our 'belief'. Many of the former students, teachers and administrators reveal an epoch in their lives at the RHS, PMCI and CCHS Schools. They provide us with a solid message – undeterredness by parents to educate their children. Superb effort Adarsh. I must commend you. It reminds me of a quote from the illustrious V.S. Naipaul:-

"One isn't born one's self; one is born with a mass

Of expectations, a mass of other people's ideas and you have to work through it all".

* Dennis Boodram: CFP, CLU, CF.F.C

A former student and former teacher

CHAPTER 8

Photographs of teachers, students and their schools (Rose Hall High School, the school at Port Mourant Race Course, The school at Port Mourant Comprehensive insititute and the Corentyne Comprehensive High School.)

This section reflects (in pictures) the journey of Rose Hall High School.... The first RHS, then the RHS at (Reef).... to the Port Mourant Race Course Pavillion. Then its merger with Port Mourant Comprehensive Institute to form the Corentyne Comprehensive High School. (Photos could not be obtained for the original Rose Hall High School when RHS started although innumerable attempts were made.) In this presentation each picture tells its own story followed by a description of what each picture outlines.

REFLECTIONS AT ROSE HALL HIGH SCHOOL

The following prayer was introduced by Mr. Rudra Nath and this prayer became the inspiration for the entire school........ Every morning.

PRAYER

O Living and Loving one

From Thee we come to Thee we turn

Thou art more than father and mother to us all

May thy Light guide us

And Thy Love lead us into the harmonies of Life

So that we may become responsive

To every touch of nature

To every whisper of truth

To every cry of humanity

Amen

FIRST DAY OF CLASS

The new class of 1962 had just assembled in the newly constructed wing of RHS at the reef. Optimism was in the air. The first class was English Literature for 2A Asregadoo and 2A Hari. Teachers, Haman Ben Yassim and Adarsh Kumar Hari felt that we were much better than to be merely reading the poetry of Keats and Shelley and others - though that was important. It was critical that we use our innate creativity to write our own. Our first task was to write a poem about our school in 8, 6, 8, 6 lines. I can still hear Ben sounding off the scheme rhythmically to make sure we got it:

Do dum do dum do dum do dum

Do dum do dum do dum

Do dum do dum do dum do dum

Do dum do dum do dum

We then set to work under the creative guidance of Ben and Adarsh. 2A Asregadoo came up with:

My school is large and newly made

Its name is Rose Hall High

For it my love will never fade

Until the day I die.

Not to be outdone, 2A Hari responded:

My school is large and beautiful

It stands along the coast

It forms a view so wonderful

Of it we all do boast.

No more than doggerel, you say? You are correct. But it was the heartfelt expression of pride and expectation in our first day of class in our new school. Greater things were ahead.

Submitted by Errol Arthur

CHAPTER 9

CLASSROOM HUMOR

Here are some funny stories that rang through the halls of RHS, PMCI and CCHS. They are expected to add a little bit of humor and why not? We welcome a laugh or two knowing that laughter is one of the best remedies for today's maladies….. It can also help reduce wrinkles.

SANICHAR'S KNOCKOUT FUNNIES

Rudra Nath:" Mr. Naidoo!"

Naidoo:"Yes Sir!"

Rudra Nath:"You were absent yesterday, Why?

Naidoo:"I was sick ,Sir.

Rudra Nath:" but I saw you with a beer in your hand at Uncle Ganga's, beer Joint.

Naidoo:"Too much of that medicine made me sick. Sir"

Rudra Nath:" Ha! Ha! Ha! Your class is waiting for you.

Naidoo: "Yes Sir".

Rawana:" What happened Gaj? Four times already this morning to the toilet.

Gaj::" Ha boy, slash…slash."

Rawana:" Why man. Why? Ha! Ha! Ha!"

Gaj:" Boy, Russian Beer and Auntie Betty's Chicken and hot pepper sauce"

FROM OTHER SOURCES: A VERY SHORT PIECE

Teacher on a literary masterpiece on literature, The Ballad of Sir Patrick Spens:

"the King sits in Dunfermline Town, drinking the blude-reid wine, oh where shall I get a skelly Skipper to sail this ship of mine"..

Student,(Bhagouti),(thinking), but a little confused:" oh ras man, this na geography, seems really different to me".

DWARKA PERSAUD'S CONTRIBUTION

Life at Rose Hall High school was not all about serious studies, we had some memorable times of fun. This little incident is one of such fun- like memories which may evoke laughter. We wore khaki short pants with light blue short sleeve shirts and a yellow tie as uniform. Imagine the boys, 16 to 18 years old, exposing their hairy legs.

Shortly before writing senior Cambridge exams we were somewhat embarrassed to go in the exam room at Chandi Singh high school in short pants. My friend, Hardutt Ramcharran, (now a Professor in economics) decided that since we may not be going back to school around the exam time he thought of 'pulling one 'on his old father in order to wear long pants while writing the overseas exam.

He told his father that Mr. Rudra Nath said that we should wear long pants for the examination. His poor father went to great financial sacrifice in order to get him long pants. After the examination was finished, myself and a few others were still going to school not knowing whether we would pass or fail. In the case of failure we may have to continue school and to re-sit the exam. Not long after Arjunen Permaul and myself and a few others were still going to school. Arjunen and myself were helping Mr. Nath to sort out, rearrange and reorganize some library books as the school was trying to establish a library.

Lo and behold, an old gray-haired man came into Mr. Nath's office, the normal Hindu greetings were exchanged: "Ram! Ram! Etc." He asked Mr. Nath in broken Creole Guyanese language,," Teach, ah wha kind a trouble and expense you put me in to get long pants". Mr Nath smilingly looked up at Permaul and me and began to laugh. The old man was surprised at Mr. Nath's reaction.

Mr. Nath asked us to tell uncle that that was not the case and that Hardat pulled one on him to get to wear long pants for the exam. The old man said:" Me gonna break his ass when he come home this afternoon". Mr.Nath said: "Uncle, do not worry with him, he will eventually use those pants to work."

We hurriedly packed the books and returned to the classroom. We told Hardat about his father and what transpired with Mr.Nath. Hardat exclaimed," Oh God, he gonna kill me ass this afternoon when I go home". The rest is history. There were many memorable incidents and issues during my three years at Rose Hall high school which left me with some lasting memories and impressions.

GANESH HARILAL'S FUNNIES

Every high school or institution has a unique history in terms of the people who serve them. Some of us may recall the funny, mischievous, and dynamic personalities at Comprehensive. Stanley Kalicharran, my classmate, was such a person. He was very affable and gregarious with a tremendous sense of humor. Stanley made us laugh all the time. With him as a classmate, attending high school was fun.

Everyday, school began with morning prayers. There were rumors that during prayers when our eyes were closed, a male teacher, our form master, would court a female teacher down the hallway. One morning, during prayers Stanley Kallicharran pretending to pray, peeked at the teacher. He saw some cavorting and began laughing. The teacher, feeling awkward and embarrassed, walked up to Stanley and questioned him. An argument broke out while we were still in prayers. Suddenly, we heard them challenging each other to fight. Both stormed out to the open school yard. The prayers were over and we were sitting gossiping about what just occurred. A few minutes passed and Stanley and the teacher returned to the classroom laughing. The situation was diffused!

At Comprehensive, we were taught physics although we had no lab. Ramkerat was the Physics teacher. In one of the lessons during the afternoon session, he taught us the physics of the pinhole camera and how it worked. When he was finished and walking away,

Stanley sitting in the back benches shouted, "Pinhole". Teacher Ramkerat turned around and demanded to know who called him, pinhole. Everyone was afraid to speak so we did not answer. A very angry Ramkerat placed the whole class in detention. This caused a crisis because the class was scheduled to go on a field trip. Principal Rudra Nath came and requested the class be released. An argument ensued but in the end Ramkerat refused to let the class go. Needless to say, we missed our field trip!

Once, Stanley took the cap of Felix, a fellow student, and hid it. After searching a while for his cap and could not find it, Felix went to the principal's office to complain. Principal, Rudra Nath came to the class to investigate. No one ratted on Stanley. Because of this all of the mail students, except Felix, were suspended for two days. We, of course, enjoyed the time off. We used one day of our suspension to "bush cook" at Port Mourant race course. We were all grateful to Stanley.

Rudra Nath was a very didactic principal. In the mornings, he will have meetings with students lining them up in military style, for inspection. While doing this, he came upon my brother, Seerinauth Harilal. He stopped, looked at him carefully and said, "You are wearing an off white shirt and not blue. Since you are not wearing the blue uniform, you have to go home". Seerinauth was wearing a washed out blue terylene shirt so he answered," Sir, this is a blue terylene shirt". Rudra Nath became angry and demanded, with an aura of authority and confidence that Seerinauth prove that his shirt is blue. Seerinauth promptly turned his shirt pocket inside out and there it was the original blue color of the shirt. Rudra Nath had no choice but to concede. He walked to the next student in the line!

WALTER RAMDEHOLL BY RAY SUNDAR

The memory is a wee bit fuzzy……… but I'll give it a try.

It was one of the most hilarious moments of my time at, Corentyne Comprehensive high school. Perhaps a snapshot in time.

The year was 1966. Mr. Ramdeholl had just ascended the coveted Compri throne--- the principalship.

My classroom was on the first floor of the big, old, green, dilapidated building. In walked Mr. Ramdeholl, a shortish gentleman – the new Economics teacher.

As he was writing on the chalkboard after exchanging some initial pleasantries, one of the students seated to my immediate left, uttered in a low voice, these now infamous words,"Ras man, Mutt gone, Jeff come." Boisterous laughter, seemingly uncontrollable, erupted in the classroom.

Mr. Ramdeholl made an instantaneous 180° turn, asking, perhaps incredulously,   "who said that?" Not a boy or girl stirred as complete silence enveloped the classroom.

Mr. Ramdeholl, assuming a belligerent stance, slapped the table with the wild cane he brought and repeated the question. Perhaps the crackling sound of the wild cane had canethe desired effect……. rather sheepishly, and perhaps, fearfully. Square, a student from Tain, stood up and said,"sir,me say dat,!" Mr. Ramdehol asked, "What did you say?" Square responded," Sir, me say, Ras man, Mutt gone and Jeff come." Mr. Ramdeholl reared back and burst out laughing, in the process admonishing Square to behave himself.

Oh! I do not know! Perhaps this simple, singular reaction, without any noticeable malice, endeared him to many students. Certainly, seems like he won over many students that day.

Whether or not Square was aware of the enormity of what he said I do not know. However, he became somewhat of a quasi celebrity for comparing the height of Mr. Ramdeholl (Napoleon Bonaparte comes to mind) to that of Mr. Rudra Nath, a former principal – two relatively short gentlemen who became giants in the educational sector. Kudos to Square!

EXAMINATION DAY
ERROL ARTHUR

"If you nah want cut cane fuh a livin, you better pass five subject with English and Maths". This is wha me muddah plead wid me as she spoon feed me de Phosphorene. She was sure that that woulda clear up de "brain fog" when ah sit me finals fuh de GCE examination later dat mahnin. Every student had he or she personal remedy fuh jes dat affliction. For Baljit Etwaroo it was Sanatogen – de tonic, not de powder. Ricknauth Budhu was a Nutrophos man heself. An you see dat Mahadeo Rajdhanny, he down mo dan he fair share ah fish head braff. De fish brains does mek you smart, he Ajah tell he. But I hear dat he does drink it fuh other reasons, but dat is anotha story.

Me mother exhortation wasn't idle, you know. Five subjects GCE with English and Maths was indeed we passport out ah de drudgery and hopelessness of life pon de Corentyne. It was also the least she coulda expeck fuh de sacrifice she mek to afford me and me buddy an sistah dem a secondary education. It open doors to become a teacha boy, a civil servant, or to go to de Teachers Training College, the University of Guyana or any other university. If you was a boy chile an you fail it mean you had to plant rice, cut cane, or become a loongayrah. If you was a gyurl chile it mean dat you parents had to find a boy an marry you off quick quick. De only life you had den was to cook fuh you husband and mek pickney. Dat din seem like no life to look forward to.

And, so it was that about two hundred ah we nervous souls find we self at de Belvedere Government School to sit for the first subject – English Language. You coulda see some ah we cramming at the last second. Every man jack walk with extra pens, pots of ink, lead pencils, pencil erasers, rulers, and other paraphernalia – no man din want to get ketch not prepare to handle any an every emergency dat could come up.

At the appointed hour Mr. Rawle Branco, the Head Invigilator, throw open de door to de school and tell we to come in. Mr. Branco was the retired Headmaster of St. Xavier Roman Catholic School in Port Mourant. He always carry heself with a dignified and regal demeanor. Even on a Saturday mahnin you coulda see he dress up ninety nine in he jacket an tie and stiffly starched white shirt as he ride his Raleigh bicycle to de Port Mourant market.

Some ah we enter de examination room strutting like Chunilall peacock to hide we nervousness. Some ah de other ones, who know they was guh fail walk in like cow getting lead to slaughter house.

Mr. Branco tek de stage and declare in he well- rehearsed and imperious tone dat de proceedings was about to begin. He hold up a wax-sealed brown manila envelope and pronounce dramatically: "Sealed in this envelope are the examination papers for English

Language for the General Certificate of Education. According to the rules and regulations of London University, it must be certified by one of the examinees that the seal is unbroken. I will now choose at random one student to have it so certified." And with dat, he walk over to Leon Mackoon to examine de seal and mek de certification.

Now Mr. Branco had over two hundred students to choose for dat task. He coulda choose Moses Nagamootoo, who was straight as a harrah, or Roy Beharry, a quiet fella who does like to flirt with dem girls. But, no! De man gone an pick de one student in dat room who born here on God's earth to give grief to teachers – Leon Mackoon. If ever you find any wutlissness somebody do to a teacher you just know that Leon hand was in it somehow.

Leon look intently at the envelope, din say a word, and allow Mr. Branco to break de seal. Is then he spring into action, " Mr. Branco, I dint see."

"What you mean, you didn't see?" asked Mr. Branco incredulously.

"I did not see that the seal was unbroken!"

"But I walked all the way over here from the stage and put the envelope right up to your eye. How can you then say you didn't see?" rejoined Mr. Branco.

Leon was now at his lawyerly best, "Mr. Branco, London University specifically and categorically states that an examinee must certify that the seal on the envelope is unbroken. It does not say that the examinee must just be shown the envelope but that he must see and certify that the seal is unbroken. I did not see that the seal was unbroken and cannot so certify. Therefore this examination is illegal."

Now wherever Leon go you can expect that his posse was not

far behind. Chimed in Leo Matthews: "But Mr. Branco if de man dint see, de man dint see. You self cyan expeck de man to say he see when he dint see."

Winston Dutchin joined the line, "Tell he rass deh, Leo. If Mr. Branco bruk de seal without Leon seein, then the exam illegal. Cancel de exam and leh we go home."

By this time it was sheer pandemonium. Some students who probably feel dat they was not going to pass de exam anyway was only too glad to support Leon. Those who was prepared for de exam was quite irritated at the possibility of prolonging the agony that a postponement would entail. Some others, out of sheer wutlissniss was savoring Mr. Branco's discomfort, especially if them was some ah he former students who may have felt the wrath of he "wild cane".

By this time the crowd smell blood. Suddenly from the left come a shout, "Branco!" Mr. Branco hurry over to check it out. Total silence. Now from de right, "Branco!" Mr. Branco hurry over. Again total silence.

He imperial and dignified demeanor now desert he. "Branco! Branco! Branco! Ah tun dis side, dah side want Branco. Ah tun dah side, dis side want Branco. Wah ah you want with Branco?"

"We want you to cancel this tainted examination!" shouted Leon. Leo, Winston an de posse concurred.

Now I was really enjoyin de bacchanal when George Jhagroo, the Regional Educational Officer walk in. After listenin to Mr. Branco's explanation he declare dat de exams mus begin immediately an any man jack who had a problem with dat should send he a written complaint. He gon then tek de necessary action. The ruckus end as abruptly as how it start! As Lord Canary may have put it, it was like when Kallicharran batting, and with his score in the nineties "rain come and end de match".

You see that man Jhagroo, he ent gat no sense ah humor! Steuupppsssssss!!!

The Mangru's Edge
By Bansraj Mangru

I can now gladly mention an episode I had with Mr. Rudra Nath at Rose Hall High School. Rudra was a philosopher, moralist but a very strict disciplinarian. He tried to establish education at all costs. He made it crystal clear that all the young adults should keep their hormones in check or face the dire consequences.

I was courting my wife, Anjanie at the school during that time, but we assumed that this was done secretly. However, it seemed that Rudra had eyes all over the place. I was called to his office and was asked why I was often seen walking with Anjanie. I had to think fast. I told Mr. Nath that Anjanie was my sister with the same last name, Mangru. Surprisingly, he said, "then, Bansraj you have every right to walk with your sister"

Sometime later after graduation I invited Mr.Nath to my engagement ceremony. Boy was he surprised. He could not believe his eyes. He said," Bansraj, isn't this the Anjanie, you told me was your sister?" I said, "Yes, Mr. Nath, I did, but under the circumstance I had to. My sincerest apology. Now we both have and education and thanks to you sir." Boy, Bansraj, you certainly pulled the wool over my eyes."added Mr. Nath. "Anyway, I'm glad for you both. Congratulations!!!"

CONCLUSION

I would like to emphasize that throughout the 10+ years of our journeys through these institutions, we faced many hurdles and obstacles, but we were able to overcome them. Although the waters of our journey were not always tranquil, we were still able to transcend expectations in the field of education. Because of our outstanding results achieved by our students at the College of Preceptors, Senior Cambridge and General Certificate of Examination, 'O' level Exams, we were achieving a status never seen in the Corentyne area before and that gave us a feeling of great accomplishments and a deep sense of pride at the tremendous success we were achieving. Yes, we were proud of our achievements and what we stood for. We were also proud of our students and our teachers who sacrificed so much and who strove always to give their best.

Throughout these episodes we had a mission to fulfill – to establish a good education. Our motto was "education for all; and on this mission we had established our goal. The goal was to resurrect in our students a better hope for the future; to energize their power of reason and ambition; to guide their minds and then empower them with the salt of wisdom, knowledge, and understanding; and with a constant resolve to motivate and inspire their hearts to strive toward the essentials of a good education and to be successful in life.

The educational influence of these institutions had a significant as well as a far reaching impact on the lives of our students. Without this opportunity, thousands of our boys and girls would have been deprived of a good secondary education and would not be as successful and gratified as they are in today's world.

Through these halls of learning at RHS, PMCI and CCHS, they were taught not only to master so many subjects and to acquire a certificate in the end, but also to be nurtured with the essentials of a good life – to know more of who they are and to believe in themselves that they are the sculptors of their own destiny. A look at what they did is truly remarkable .When they were faced with adverse circumstances and situations; when the odds were against them they refused to give up. They were ready to fight and overcome, knowing that turning back would be a failure. Facing it all was there golden opportunity and their privilege to make the best use of their challenges. Their feet were cast in the education mold and they were ready to gather all the tools of learning; to work harder and more efficiently, and to aspire to be better, and to build their dream Empire.

Today, in Guyana and abroad (in the Caribbean, USA, Canada, Europe, Australia, and other countries around the world) our 'citizens of the world,' both students and teachers, are exceedingly proud of their accomplishments. They have ventured into every field of their endeavor and these ambassadors of our schools (RHS, PMCI and CCHS) have displayed great marks of distinctions. Their success stories are remarkable. Many are now boasting of their high academic achievements and their superb economic statuses. Quite a few have become millionaires, others have achieved great educational and professional statuses as Lawyers, Teachers, Professors, Engineers, Corporate heads, CPA's, RN's, BA's, MA's, PhD's, etc. It is very gratifying to behold that our grand achievers are making great inroads in the growth of their communities. They are giving themselves, and, making a significant impact in life and on lives.

Some of these successful students and teachers have tasted the honeysuckle of life and today are enjoying the accomplished lifestyles— maybe, now they can enjoy the lifestyles of the rich and famous in their little nest of associations, friends and families, and communities in which they live. It is so wonderful to know that they have not lost their true identity, nor have they forgotten from where they came. They seem to retain their original uniqueness, yet always blazing towards higher plateaus of life. Today, they are transmitting to their children, grandchildren, and associates their virtues, ideologies, educational values, ambition, and unique traits of themselves, their working philosophies, and doctrines. In short, they are establishing a new imprint of the older lessons of life they learned and are encouraging others on this great path of educational stability and growth, knowing that this path gave them so much, and which was able to enrich, enhance and establish their lives learned from these institutions --- RHS, PMCI and CCHS.

GLOSSARY

Ajah Paternal grandfather

Acqueduct A construction which enables two sets of water to cross at a

   particular point without mixing

Afro-GuyaneseDescendants whose forefathers came from Africa

Amerindian-GuyaneseGuyanese whose fore-fathers were the first inhabitants

   of the country

Bacchanal Pandemonium / structured confusion

Bound- yardA slum area with logies (huts) where East Indian

   Immigrants were essentially bound to live the

   rest of their lives

BraffBroth

BBP Black Bush Polder--- one of the largest agricultural schemes in Guyana and

   one of the largest in the English-speaking Caribbean.

CCHSmerged entity of RHS (Rose Hall High School) and PMCI

   (Port Mourant Comprehensive Institute)

Chinese- GuyaneseDescendants whose fore-fathers came from China

CyanCan't

Divali   Known as, "the festival of lights" in certain regions of India.

It's a five-day festival and is one of the most important

festivals of the year. It's celebrated in families who perform

traditional activities together in their homes. Divali is celebrated

in other parts of the world where Indians live.

GAWU Guyanese Agricultural Workers Union

Gyurl chile Girl child

Harrah Arrow

HindiLanguage spoken by the Hindus

Indentured ImmigrantPersons who work as laborers for a contracted period at a stipulated wage

Indo-GuyanesePeople in Guyana whose fore-fathers came from India as indentured

immigrants to work on the Sugar Estates.

Jook, JukTo insert or plant in the ground

Kokers Also called locks which were used for drainage purposes on the sugar

estates and for keeping out the sea water during high tides.

Loungera (Loongayrah)   One who goes from place to place having no purpose—a wanderer

Logies Long wooden ranges which were living quarters built on the Sugar

Estates for laborers.

Mamoo	Maternal brother.

Maube	A local drink made from the Maubee bark.

Overseer	European employee on the Sugar Estates who lived in the Senior

Staff Compound and who was in charge of gangs of sugar workers

Pandit	Hindu Priest

Phagwah	Also called Holi is a colorful and boisterous Hindu spring festival in

India. It is known as the "festival of colors" where people smear each other

with colorful powders and shower each other with colorful water. There is

no restriction to caste, sex and age. Personal differences are ignored—it's a

time for revelry.

Pickney	Children

Portuguese-Guyanese	Descendants in Guyana whose forefathers went to Guyana as indentured

Immigrants from Madeira

PNC	The People's National Party --- A political party in Guyana under Forbes

Burnham. This Party was formed when Forbes Burnham in1957 broke away

. from the PPP.

PPP A political party (People's Political Party) headed by Dr. Cheddi Jagan

who became the first president of Guyana and who brought independence

to Guyana.

Satsang Hindu gathering for religious worship

U.G.University of Guyana.

WutlissnessWickedness

Yagna Hindu religious worship lasting over a number of days, usually three

to seven days

Teerat is a religious observance through a series of purification rites directing man

man towards the liberation of the soul. It is celebrated as a bath in the river

or sea or in the Ganges regarded as the Mother who cleanses man from sin.

DISCLOSURE

All Information presented in the preceding pages were obtained from sources deemed reliable—the author, former students and teachers and distinguished members of the community who were there thoughtout the struggles of the schools. Although the data obtained are believed to be authentic and correct no one can, including the author, verify that all the materials presented are true and correct knowing that this history took place over 50 years ago and that the narratives were obtained from personal recall. However, this history is written to give a true perspective of the past, yet, to reveal what actually happened

www.ingramcontent.com/pod-product-compliance
Lightning Source LLC
Chambersburg PA
CBHW070920120626
46546CB00001B/337